Praise for *Life Visioning*

"Michael Beckwith's new book, *Life Visioning*, is a game changer. It is not only filled with deep spiritual insight; it provides a practical, step-by-step system that can help you enter what I have called the 'miracle universe.' Life can be easier, clearer, and more inspiring than we humans have ever through possible, and now the precise information for living in this reality is surfacing in our time. This book helps us all get in alignment with the true spiritual design of the universe."

JAMES REDFIELD
Author of *The Celestine Prophecy* series

"This inspired and brilliant work gives us the understanding and tools of Sacred Psychology. Michael Beckwith offers the potent and profound methods of his Life Visioning Process, a meta technology of consciousness that takes the reader through the stages of his or her own expanded possibilities. Radically original in concept and design, this book offers a unique evolutionary path to the birth of a new humanity."

JEAN HOUSTON, PHD
Author of *A Passion for the Possible*

"*Life Visioning* is a master work from a master teacher. Michael Beckwith writes directly from his life experience as a spiritual pioneer to the heart and soul of every person, no matter what the situation or immediate condition. He guides all of us through deep contact with the evolutionary impulse within, the dynamic source of creativity. Through his teachings, we are able to release our illusions of separation and fear, and invite the life process to animate and guide us."

BARBARA MARX HUBBARD
Author of *Essence: The Shift from Ego to Essence*

Praise for Michael Bernard Beckwith

"I greatly admire what Michael is doing to bring about the Beloved community, which is certainly what my dear husband worked and ultimately gave his life for." **CORETTA SCOTT KING**

"As a modern day sage, Michael truly captures the magnitude of the divinity in today's humanity and simply catches it on fire! I thank him for his soulful expression and masterful contribution to the planet." **DR. SUE MORTER**
Founder of Morter Health Center

"I love Dr. Beckwith's insights and brilliance so thoroughly that I buy, listen, and re-listen to every one of his talks. He has convinced me that we can think in solutions rather than problems."
MARK VICTOR HANSEN
Originator of *Chicken Soup* series

"Reverend Michael's inspiring life story helps individuals on the path to greater lovingkindness, compassion, and altruism for the sake of all sentient beings and world peace."
TALHUM KHEN RINPOCHE
GESHE KKACHEN LOBZANG TSETAN
Abbot of Tashi Lhumpo Monastery in exile, Bylakuppe, India

"I am grateful to be a recipient of Michael's generosity of spirit and love. What a blessing!" **IYANLA VANZANT**
Author of *Tapping the Power Within*

"The work of Dr. Beckwith may be unprecedented in American history for its spiritual effectiveness and its humanitarian inclusiveness interracially, interculturally, interdenominationally."
DR. LAWRENCE E. CARTER
Dean of Morehouse College Martin Luther King Chapel
and author of *Ethical Global Options*

lifevisioning

Also by Michael Bernard Beckwith

Books

Spiritual Liberation: Fulfilling Your Soul's Potential
40 Day Mind Fast Soul Feast
The Answer Is You
Inspirations of the Heart
A Manifesto of Peace
TranscenDance

Audio with Sounds True

The Answer Is You
Connecting with the Overflow
Life Visioning
The Life Visioning Process
Living from the Overflow
True Abundance
Your Place of Power
Your Soul's Evolution

Sound of Agape Music
Rickie Byars Beckwith

Discography

From Within
I Found a Deeper Love
In the Land of I AM
Pray for Me
Soul Fulfilling
Supreme Inspiration

Book

Let My Soul Surrender

Agape International Choir Discography

I Release and I Let Go
I Walk in the Love of God
Spirit Says to Sing
Live from Agape: Volume 1–23 Songs of Rhythm & Joy

lifevisioning

A Transformative Process
for Activating Your Unique Gifts
and Highest Potential

Michael Bernard Beckwith

SOUNDS TRUE
Boulder, Colorado

Sounds True, Inc.
Boulder, CO 80306

Published 2013

The epigraphs used at the beginning of each chapter are lyrics from
songs written by Michael Bernard Beckwith and Rickie Byars Beckwith.
Published and copyright Eternal Dance Music. All rights reserved.

Cover and book design by Dean Olson
Cover photo by Carl Studna

Printed in the United States of America

Library of Congress Cataloging-in-Publication Data

Beckwith, Michael Bernard.
  Life visioning : a transformative process for activating your unique
gifts and highest potential / Michael Bernard Beckwith.
     p. cm.
  ISBN 978-1-60407-629-5
  1. Spiritual life. 2. Self-realization—Religious aspects. I. Title.

  BL624.B3938 2012
  204'.4—dc23
                                          2011033404
  ISBN 978-1-62203-050-7
  Ebook ISBN 978-1-60407-661-5

10 9 8 7 6 5

To the love and muse of my life, Rickie Byars Beckwith, my wife; to my parents, Alice and Francis Beckwith, who have graced my life with their generous, loving hearts; to my children, Kiilu and Micaela, and my grandchildren, whom I love beyond words. And a big shout-out to Georgia and Stephan, Rickie's children, who are part of my wonderful family.

Contents

Foreword | ix

Introduction: **How to Become "Yes!"** | 1

PART ONE: EVOLVING THROUGH THE STAGES

Chapter 1: **The Universality of Visioning** | 13

Chapter 2: **The Four Stages
of Evolutionary Growth** | 27

Chapter 3: **Stage One:
Victim Consciousness** | 39

Chapter 4: **Stage Two:
Manifester Consciousness** | 57

Chapter 5: **To Connect,
Must We Disconnect?** | 83

Chapter 6: **Stage Three:
Channel Consciousness** | 91

Contents

Chapter 7: **Stage Four:**
Being Consciousness | 111

PART TWO: THE LIFE VISIONING PROCESS

Chapter 8: **The Dark Night**
of the Soul | 125

Chapter 9: **Preparing the Ground**
of Consciousness | 133

Chapter 10: **The Art and Science**
of Visioning | 145

Chapter 11: **Integrating the Vision into**
Our Life Structures | 159

Epilogue: **A View from the Heart** | 181

Acknowledgments | **187**

Credits | **189**

About the Author | **191**

Foreword

CRISIS IGNITES EVOLUTION. The collective nature of current global crises is a clear sign that humanity is poised on the brink of a radical evolutionary upheaval. Exciting research from the frontiers of science emphasizes that we are, each and all, active participants in what will amount to be the greatest adventure in human history — conscious evolution.

In support of our evolutionary destiny, I am honored to introduce Michael Beckwith's *Life Visioning,* a life-changing technology that can profoundly influence the fate of human civilization.

Science now acknowledges that we are deep into the sixth mass extinction of life on planet Earth. Unfortunately, that extinction includes the fate of human civilization. The five previous extinctions, one of which wiped out the dinosaurs, were due to physical factors such as comets or asteroids hitting the Earth. The current mass extinction, according to science, is directly attributable to human behavior.

The beliefs we hold about ourselves and the role we play in the world have undermined the environment and are destroying the web of life. For almost two hundred years, modern science has been the source of the "truths" that shape our worldview. The cultural story created from these truths is now leading us to our own extinction. If we want our world to change, then what we think about our world and more specifically ourselves—our "story"— must change first.

The good news is that frontier science is shattering old myths and rewriting the fundamental beliefs that shape culture and the fate of human civilization. Recent discoveries offer civilization a compelling and hopeful new story, one so "out of the box" of conventional wisdom that even science is having a hard time accepting its implications. The premise of science's new story is one of harmony and relatedness, of life and love.

In order to effectively contribute to our evolution and outgrow the threatening global challenges, we must first shed our image of being helpless victims and learn the truth as to who we really are. Through conventional science we have been led to believe that humans are genetically programmed biochemical automatons, powerless in controlling the unfolding of our lives. In contrast, recent advances in frontier science now offer a radically "new biology."

As I write in my book *The Biology of Belief,* discoveries in quantum physics and cell biology now invoke a fundamental role for *spirit* (referred to as the *field* in physics) and mind as the creative forces that control behavior and genetics. The newly described biological pathways illuminate the mechanisms by which our thoughts, attitudes, and beliefs create the conditions of our body and our experiences in the external world.

Most people are understandably skeptical of this conclusion simply because their own lives rarely match the wishes and desires they hold in their minds. Exacerbating the problem is that the much-touted effort of changing one's life through "positive thinking" (controlling the mind) is rarely successful.

Fortunately, new research provides empowering insights that resolve this perplexing issue and offer us an opportunity to create Heaven on Earth. The secret to our problem is that we have failed to fully understand the nature and interaction between the mind's two functionally different subdivisions, the *subconscious* and the *(self-) conscious minds.*

The *conscious mind* is the seat of the personal identity we associate with "self," source or *spirit.* It is the thinking, creative mind that contemplates and acts upon our wishes, desires, and aspirations. The conscious mind is not time-bound, for its thought processing allows us to relive past experiences or leap into visions of the future.

In contrast, the *subconscious mind* is neither a thinking nor an especially creative mind. Its proficiency is that it is an unimaginably powerful record-playback mechanism, a million times more powerful than the conscious mind.

The subconscious mind primarily engages habits, preprogrammed reactive behaviors acquired from genetic instincts and life experiences.

The fundamental behavioral programs in our subconscious minds were acquired during the formative period between gestation and six years of age. Now here's the catch—these life-shaping subconscious programs are direct downloads derived from observing our primary teachers: our parents, siblings, and local community. Unfortunately, as psychologists are keenly aware, many of the perceptions we acquire about ourselves in this formative period are expressed as limiting and self-sabotaging beliefs.

The subconscious mind's activities are always fixed in the present moment and it does not readily discern a past or future. When the conscious mind is engaged in thought, operationally, it is not being observant of the present moment. By default, our behavior is then managed by the ever-vigilant subconscious mind. An important understanding is that we are generally unaware of our subconscious behaviors when we play them, since our conscious minds are not present or observing ourselves at these times.

So what is the reason as to why our lives don't match our conscious wishes and desires? According to neuroscientists, we only use our conscious mind about 5 percent of the time in controlling our lives. Therefore, most of our decisions, actions, emotions, and behavior are derived from the programs in the subconscious mind.

Since the fundamental behavioral patterns in the subconscious mind are primarily derived from others, it becomes clear that we are not living *our* lives, we are living *other* people's lives. Adding insult to injury, we engage these limiting, disempowering behaviors because our conscious minds are not present, and as a consequence we are generally unaware our actions are self-sabotaging.

What would life be like if we could keep our conscious minds present, a state called "mindfulness," without defaulting to subconscious programs? Most readers have actually experienced such a time; it was when we fell head-over-heels in love with someone. Referred to as the honeymoon period, most remember it as a time when they were exuberantly healthy and happy, filled with abundant energy, and life was so beautiful they couldn't wait for the next day. In truth it was as if we were experiencing Heaven on Earth.

The honeymoon period lasts till life gets so busy that our conscious minds begin to drift as our thoughts begin to focus on life strategies. That's when relationship-sabotaging behaviors, formerly hidden in the inactive subconscious mind, begin to be expressed.

Regardless of its duration, the honeymoon's Heaven-on-Earth experience was not an accident. It was the direct consequence of living from your conscious mind's wishes and desires. It is only when our invisible dysfunctional familial and cultural behaviors programmed in the subconscious begin to be expressed that our lives become derailed.

One of the most important points to make is that limiting subconscious programs are not fixed, unchangeable behaviors. We have the ability to rewrite disempowering beliefs and in the process take control of our lives. Just imagine if your subconscious mind was programmed with the same behaviors held in the conscious mind: We would be able to experience a perpetual Heaven for as long as we live!

Now that we know what science is telling us about the true nature of human nature, what do we do about it? How do we liberate ourselves from our personal and collective programming of limitation?

To change subconscious programs requires the activation of processes other than engaging in a running dialogue with the subconscious mind, especially since there is no one in the machine-like subconscious mind to dialogue with. The primary mechanism to acquire new habits in the subconscious mind after the age of six is through the use of repetitive behaviors, hence the need for a "practice." Evolution—like Heaven—is not a destination, but a practice.

What practices can we adopt on a daily basis that remind us of who we truly are? I find that one of the more effective tools in rewriting our limiting beliefs is Michael Beckwith's *Life Visioning*.

The Life Visioning Process™ (LVP) supports us by drawing our attention to the ways in which we sabotage our success and reveals that these saboteurs aren't inherent—they are simply the consequence of the disempowering behavioral programs we acquired in our youth. Beckwith's Life Visioning Process focuses on the mindsets and behavior patterns that must be released, as well as on cultivating new behaviors that allow us to regain creative control over our lives.

As we recognize our ability to change our programming, we evolve from passive victims to responsible co-creators.

Foreword

A miraculous healing awaits this planet once we accept our new responsibility to collectively tend the Garden. Michael Beckwith's *Life Visioning* offers people an opportunity to truly own this belief in their hearts and minds and begin living from these truths. This important contribution will help our world emerge from darkness in what will amount to a consciousness-based spontaneous evolution for humans, by humans.

—Bruce H. Lipton, PhD

Introduction

How to Become "Yes!"

THROUGHOUT OUR FORMATIVE years and into adulthood we are given prescriptions, admonitions, exhortations, and instructions for doing our life, yet little or nothing about becoming our authentic self and living our life purpose. For that, an introduction is required, which is the ultimate purpose of the Life Visioning Process™ (LVP) and this book. Through visioning, you will be introduced to the You of you. And the moment you come into your own being you will say "yes" to it, all of it.

As a way of inviting you into the journey, I'd like to take you back with me to when and how Life Visioning originated. LVP was literally a homebirth that took place in the privacy of my meditation room, followed by its public debut in my living room. But first, a brief history. On May 18, 1985, I graduated from the Ernest Holmes College School of Ministry, and on July 1, 1985, I became a licensed minister in the United Church of Religious

Science (recently renamed Centers for Spiritual Living), which is a part of the larger New Thought movement. At the time, I was a full-time licensed prayer practitioner and spiritual counselor, on the faculty of the school of ministry from which I graduated, and director of training in its prayer ministry. Outside of that environment, I conducted my own seminars and workshops.

Even though I was a licensed minister and was invited to speak at various spiritual communities, I did not have my own church. And that was just fine with me! I had my weekends off, which worked just great for a father with two young children and someone who greatly enjoyed their personal downtime. After all, wasn't I already giving enough time to supporting others through my ministerial calling? A rhetorical question, obviously, a justification for resisting that voice within that kept urging me to surrender, to step out and embrace the calling I allowed myself to acknowledge only for fleeting seconds. In case you're wondering why I graduated from ministerial school if I wasn't planning on having a church, it's really pretty simple: I love being in a learning atmosphere. And, for clarification's sake, being a minister is about more than having one's own congregation.

Then came the invitation—a rude intruder into the even tenor of my days. A spiritual community at which I had been a guest speaker a few times expressed their interest in having me as their senior minister, a position for which I had to candidate along with other applicants. When their selection committee reviewed my credentials, I learned in a roundabout way that they didn't want to submit my name to their board of trustees, who were entrusted with making the final selection. It seemed that my being African American would be problematic in conservative Orange County. Now, I enjoyed a good relationship with the congregation, so this callousness and bigotry came as a hurtful shock. The short version is that I spent a good deal of time working on forgiving those involved, removed my name from the list of candidates, sincerely blessed everyone, and lovingly moved on.

Having done so, however, did nothing to silence the voice that continued to echo in my meditations, during times of affirmative prayer, self-contemplation, even in the shower—any time there was a moment of silence there it would be, announcing that the ministry was my life purpose. During that time of great resistance, I was often reminded of a verse from the poem "The Hound of Heaven," by Francis Thompson, wherein he shares his personal and mystical story of trying to hide from God:

> *I fled Him down the nights and down the days*
> *I fled Him down the arches of the years*
> *I fled Him down the labyrinthine ways*
> *Of my own mind, and in the midst of tears*
> *I hid from Him, and under running laughter.*
> *From those strong feet that followed, followed after*
> *But with unhurrying chase and unperturbed pace,*
> *Deliberate speed, majestic instancy,*
> *They beat and a Voice beat,*
> *More instant than the feet:*
> *All things betray thee who betrayest me.*

Eventually, I surrendered. And when I did, I became the "yes" to what was seeking to emerge in, through, and as my life. Upon bellowing out this "yes" in front of my meditation altar, what is today known as the Life Visioning Process was birthed.

It all began with this simple question: "What is my life purpose; what is seeking to emerge in, through, and as my life?" My inner tone was adamant. I was determined not to leave my meditation seat without receiving an answer. That may sound like an arrogant gauntlet to throw down before God, but the truth is there was within me a fierce determination to live nothing less than my true calling in life. Besides, according to many spiritual authorities, God has been handling spiritual tantrums since the beginning of time!

When I intuitively caught that I was to found my own spiritual community, it was no longer possible to retreat into any false humility about not being worthy, adequately spiritually prepared, or any other excuses. So I began right where I was, confident and grateful for the clarity of what was revealed and every step in the process that graced me into that place of awareness.

In that spontaneous first visioning, I caught that I was to call together a team of like-minded individuals who would become "visioneers," and that together we would midwife what was required to support the vision's next expression. That sounded pretty wild, yet workable. So I brought together in my living room a team comprised of colleagues, clients, and friends for our first group visioning.

I led them into the first step, which is to meditate so that the mind and heart may merge into a feeling tone of unconditional love. With our hearts now opened, I explained the second step, which is to place a question before the intuitive faculty of the Higher Self, which in this case was: "What is the highest expression of a spiritual community devoted to being a beneficial presence on the planet?"

We continued to meditate upon that question and after about twenty minutes we began sharing what came through and recorded it for later reference. (I recommend you also keep a journal near you when visioning so that you may capture your responses, feelings, and insights.) We had a collective realization that it was time for a trans-denominational, culturally inclusive, creative community whose teachings would encompass the universal truth principles of the world's spiritual traditions about our connection to Source and the laws governing the universe.

We then went to the third step and asked, "What qualities must we cultivate to manifest this vision?" This question is pivotal, because we cannot manifest what we are not willing to embody in consciousness. So, in effect, we were asking what we needed to become in order to be in integrity with the vision. The fourth step was to ask, "What qualities must be let go in order to manifest this vision?" followed by the fifth step, "What qualities do we already possess that will serve this vision?" Before sharing the revelations of steps three through five, we went directly into the sixth step of giving a collective "yes" to what came through, followed by the seventh step of expressing gratitude for the vision and what it would take to bring it into manifestation.

Reminiscing on that incredible evening of catching the vision for what is now the Agape International Spiritual Center, the joy is as tangible today as it was then. It brings a smile to my heart when I recollect the innocence of the moment when, at the end of the day, our financial resources to launch Agape added up to a grand total of $17. We weren't at all discouraged. On the contrary, our spiritual resources were unlimited!

In November 1986, Agape International held its first Sunday service. Twenty-six years later, we have expanded our ministries, departments, humanitarian outreach programs, classes, and staff to support our 10,000-strong local community and thousands of worldwide friends via live video streaming. Vision teams continue to lead us every step of the way. We've never stopped saying "yes!", and the vision just keeps on growing, thriving, and evolving.

Standing in Your Own "Yes"

The Life Visioning Process is a life-changing spiritual technology of conscious participation in the evolution of your consciousness. Whether you are now ready to step into the highest vision for your life or are endeavoring to ready yourself, visioning is a trustworthy guide and ally on your life path.

I urge you to keep in mind that visioning is not a personal delivery system for dropping at your doorstep the baubles of the world. It's about the evolution of who and what you are as a unique, individualized emanation of Source and what you have come on the planet to learn, express, and contribute. It's a way of providing yourself with tangible evidence that you are not here to be a passive bystander or spectator, nor to be blindly pulled along by society's ever-changing tides. Visioning is an adventure into your own deepest Self to discover there all the gifts, talents, skills, and requisite qualities of consciousness to live a most excellent life, a life of YES.

A Map of the Journey

Our venture begins with chapter 1, which explores the terrain of our eight fundamental life structures of ego, belief, relationship, health, finances, livelihood, spirituality, and community, and how the application of Life Visioning replaces a sense of lack, limitation, anxiety, and worry with a consciousness of genuine trust in the fundamental goodness of the universe and our own Self. You will learn about the five foundational qualities for practicing visioning and how to develop your own intuitive voice.

After becoming grounded in the basic principles of visioning, we move into chapter 2, where we are introduced to the Four Stages of Evolutionary Growth. Chapters 3, 4, 5, and 6 offer an in-depth description of the stages, a glimpse of which follows.

Stage One describes individuals living in Victim Consciousness, a mind-set that claims that things outside of oneself are responsible for our life circumstances, be it God, the devil, parents, mates, teachers—anything that keeps us from accepting self-responsibility for our life.

Stage Two identifies individuals who are immersed in Manifester Consciousness, using the laws of manifestation to acquire all the things they are convinced will make them happy. While they are taking self-responsibility for what shows up in their life materially, they have not entered their inner sanctuary to discover there the real treasures they seek by amassing materially.

Stage Three begins our entry into a consciousness of living "in the zone" of attunement with universal principle. Stage Four describes the mystical union of oneness with Source while fully participating in all that it means to be fully alive to our human incarnation.

Many powers beyond our individual ego lead us to our deepest purpose, and sometimes that walk includes moments, days, or months of walking in seeming darkness. These are the times when we find no succor from the God of our understanding or those around us. In chapter 8 we learn what it is to incubate in this void as a preparation for giving birth to a greater reality in and for our life. We are led into a realization that occupying this spot of extreme discomfort is exactly what is needed for the next step in our evolution.

Chapter 9 supports us to till the ground of consciousness through an understanding of the difference between visualizing and visioning, a requisite for moving into chapter 10, which gives instruction for practicing the Life Visioning Process. Chapter 11 takes us back to the eight life structures and how to integrate into them what is revealed during LVP.

A Source Beyond Ego, a Grace Beyond Luck

There is a life occurrence or a sequence of events unique to each of us that breaks through our self-imposed limitations, our egoic self-will, beckoning the Authentic Self to come forward and announce itself to us. Whether you credit it to karma or that which seeks to emerge through us, the wisdom in this grace knows exactly what conditions will cause us to exclaim, "Enough is enough. I give my consent to my next level of growth." We then set out to identify the qualities we must acquire when the truth is just the opposite: we are already fully equipped with what it takes to live the highest vision for our life. All we have to do is tap into it, to discover it within ourselves and put it into action. Visioning shines the light upon our inner treasure house, illuminating our natural wisdom, joy, compassion, intelligence, love, tranquility, creativity, and generosity.

It is a source beyond ego that provides the inner guidance that will lead us to transcending our current limitations. It lets us know we face nothing alone, that we are indeed carried by the Creator-Life walking in our feet, working through our hands, beating our hearts, and breathing through our breath. This Great Mystery is the motivating power within the Life Visioning Process. It is the underlying urge to evolve into our innate wholeness.

May each and every one of us say "yes" to accepting our life purpose, which is born out of love, thrives in love, and merges in union with love's source.

Part One

Evolving Through the Stages

Chapter 1

The Universality
of Visioning

*The song that you've been holding back
is the cause of your heartache.
Don't wait!
You've got to sing your song as if
your whole life depends on it.*

WITHIN OUR CORE SELF is an indelible blueprint of
unrivaled individuality—the singular being that each of us
exists to express. In this three-dimensional movie called
"Life" there are no stand-ins, body doubles, or understud-
ies—no one can fill in for us by proxy! Realization of this
truth alone eliminates the need to imitate, conform, limit,
or betray our loyalty to the originality of Self. Imagine the
relief of removing your carefully crafted masks fashioned
by societal forms of conditioning and instead responding

to what comes into your experience directly from your Authentic Self. One of the first principles to honor in your relationship with yourself is to respect and trust your own inner voice. This form of trust is the way of the heart, the epitome of well-being.

The brilliant Transcendentalist Ralph Waldo Emerson wisely observed that "Every man has this call of the power to do somewhat unique, and no man has any other call." His words confirm the fact that each of us is a unique, individualized emanation of Source, here to discover and release our inner splendor.

While it's a well-accepted fact that we create our way of being in the world, sometimes individuals balk at this notion because they would rather give parents, other individuals, God, or circumstances responsibility for their lives being as they are. Self-responsibility separates humans from the rest of Earth's inhabitants because of our capacity to self-contemplate, to consciously participate in cultivating an awakened consciousness, which raises existential questions relevant to being a spiritual being having a human incarnation. For example: What is my ideal livelihood at this state of my evolution? How can I move into forgiveness and heal my relationship with my parents? Are there really laws governing the universe that I can work with? What really happens after death? Why do I feel that I've lived before? Is there a difference between being spiritual and being religious?

There are countless sources to which we can turn for answers, including books, seminars, talk shows, the Web and social media, gurus, religious institutions, motivational speakers, and friends. Even so, what might you discover if you reverse the searchlight from external, exogenous sources and defer to your internal, endogenous capacity? The Life Visioning Process is a practice for becoming more deeply acquainted with yourself and for using what you discover as rich material for taking your next evolutionary leap in consciousness. LVP is a universal method that complements any existing spiritual or psychological practices in which you currently participate. In fact, you may find that it enhances your practices as you vision for the next step in your unfoldment, which may guide you to either drop or include a particular practice, or deepen in those you are currently practicing.

You Say Indigenous, I Say Endogenous

You can describe your indigenous heritage, but did you know that you are an endogenous being? The word "endogenous" comes from the Greek *endo,* which means "inside," and *genous,* meaning "producing." We all produce from the inside out. Earth and other planets are also considered endogenous because they cause continents to migrate; they trigger earthquakes and other acts of nature from their inner core. Likewise, our insights, intuitive hits, or strong emotional reactions are endogenous because they originate from inner states of consciousness influenced by our perceptions, insights, beliefs, notions, convictions, and reference points. Thus we are constantly fashioning our interiority and impacting the externality of our behavior and life circumstances.

We live in a friendly universe that doesn't require us to plead or beg for its graces. Grace is the givingness of Spirit. Some may call it answered prayer or the fundamental goodness present in the universe. Even during times when prayer appears to go unanswered or we are not lifted out of challenging circumstances, the unconditional love of Spirit is ever-present; it is not fickle, giving to some and withholding from others, giving now but not then. Although this may challenge our faith, there are karmic laws at play and other answers that the human mind cannot wrap itself around.

Recognizing the spectrum of life's possibilities and responding to them is where the juice is. Visioning enables you to see the invisible and hear the inaudible—in other words, that which is beneath the surface of the five senses. Visioning is an endogenous practice that sensitizes and utilizes the inner sixth sense of intuition and allows us to evolve into a direct knowing without the process of reasoning.

Pain Pushes Until the Vision Pulls

It is said that suffering is the great awakener. Human beings do not necessarily change voluntarily. Habits are stubborn. Many times we must hit bottom and experience great pain, which then becomes the impetus for genuine transformation. In other words, pain pushes us until a larger vision pulls us. When we choose to remain stagnant, pain will be our companion—not to inflict hurt, but to transmit a message that we are living in too small an inner world. We haven't yet recognized that pain's message is that we are ready to take the next step in our evolution.

Life Visioning gently leads you into an intuitive perception of a larger vision and reveals the steps required for its manifestation. You then understand experientially that pain doesn't have to be the impetus for your evolutionary growth.

You have taken an incarnation to awaken the enlightened expression of who you are and, while you're gracing the planet, to deliver your talents, gifts, and skills as your unique contribution to the world. The purpose of visioning is not simply about the narrow confines of personal fulfillment; it is an expansion of consciousness into the realization of your true Self.

How Life Visioning Affects Our Life Structures

Visioning is for those who are genuinely interested in breaking any agreements they have consciously or unconsciously made with mediocrity and replacing them with stability and excellence in what I refer to as our eight life structures: ego, belief, relationship, health, finances, livelihood, spirituality, and community.

Ego cannot be annihilated, but it can be tamed. It's vital to any endeavor to embody a healthy sense of self. A healthy ego focuses on creativity rather than competition. It drops notions of both superiority and inferiority. It remains confident and teachable.

Our evolving beliefs eventually lead us to the discovery of the universal principles governing the universe and our own life. When we come to the realization that we create the world we believe in, we are ready to work consciously with the laws of co-creation.

Relationship is about our ability to maturely connect to others in intimate partnership, friendship, family, and the larger community. Relationships are an opportunity to enter a field of unconditional love and compassion for ourselves and others.

Health of the body temple supports us in fulfilling our purpose, in living our vision. Good health supplies the vibrant energy required for the body's cells to replicate themselves so that we may function at our creative peak.

We seek to feel safe beyond the survival level and have been conditioned to believe that money assures this for us. Our financial structure becomes stabilized when we realize that money is energy, and that when we circulate energy in the form of money it cycles back to us. It is beneficial to be financially stable because when we are not distracted by financial stress our energy may be channeled to our spiritual practices and creatively living our vision.

Livelihood or employment goes hand in hand with our financial life structure in that when we perform work that fully utilizes our talents, gifts, and skills there is a greater possibility that we will manifest an income equal to how brightly we allow our light to shine.

Spirituality is comprised of those practices which attune us to Source and awaken us to peace, harmony, compassion, joy, bliss, wisdom—all the qualities inherent within us. Visioning supports us in listening within and being receptive to the spiritual teachings that will support us in taking the next evolutionary step in our unfoldment.

Community is about generosity of the heart, and it involves a realization of humanity's interconnection, which births within us a desire to be a beneficial presence on the planet through compassionate action and selfless service.

Every life structure is receptive to the evolutionary impress of the Life Visioning Process. When you apply the inquiry aspect of LVP (described in chapter 10), your receptivity is activated. Instead of problem-solving with the mind alone, deeper revelations occur that infuse your life structures with harmony, stability, and fulfillment.

Nothing Replaces Real-Life Experience

For over twenty-five years my practice of LVP has convinced me that that we live in an atmosphere infused with spiritual prototypes, perfect ideas that are shot from the mind of Love-Intelligence, the Universal Presence which cannot be described yet is felt through its qualities of unconditional love, beauty, compassion, grace, joy. Everything from the creation of an exquisite musical composition, a program to eliminate global warming, the invention of an electric car, the creation of the social media, to the magnetic pull of lovers toward each other—all these exist because individuals opened their consciousness, made themselves receptive to the inflow of intuition. For every project, every business endeavor, every invention, every relationship, there is limitless creativity waiting to come into expression through us.

You may vision individually, with a partner, or in a group. Visioning is applicable in multiple environments: businesses, performing arts, workshops, study circles, spiritual communities, service organizations—anywhere a vision and mission is being developed, expanded, or implemented. There is an acceleration and fortification of intention, vision, and manifestation that occurs through the contagion of group consciousness. And yet it all begins in the individual consciousness of each participant who is contributing to the collective whole.

When visioning, your life exposes itself to you. In other words, if you are willing to remain objective, you will be able to discern, without judgment, what is required to evolve into the fullest expression of yourself. You will stop struggling against yourself; rather, you draw comfort through the openness and receptivity of your own heart's longing to fully live your unique romance with Life. Visioning is a fine-tuning of the inner ear to the needs of the heart and soul.

The Five Foundational Qualities for Practicing Life Visioning

The Life Visioning Process is an inner technology set in motion by five inherent qualities: intention or willingness, receptivity or reverential alertness, acceptance of and surrender to what is revealed, the self-discipline to take action on what is revealed, and gratitude that we already have all that we need to take the next step in our evolution. When we cultivate the five foundational qualities that enhance practice of LVP, we open the door to vitalizing the mind, heart, and consciousness in ways that successfully motivate us to accelerate and accept the new into our life.

Before we begin our exploration of the five foundational qualities, I want to emphasize that it is important not to tense up or constrict the heart when we find ourselves coming up short in certain areas. It is the ego that tends to obsess over the myth of perfection, not the heart or inner spirit. It's worth repeating that the main point is to start right where you are, confident that you are not alone in your journey, that you are accompanied by an Ineffable Presence called grace. Trusting in this grace loosens our tight grip on the ego. Trust is embedded in our neurons and gives us the fortitude and courage we may not have realized is already ours. So despite the projections and judgments you may cast upon yourself, just take it all to the altar of your inner practice and know that grace is a constant companion throughout your evolutionary journey.

The Potency of a Willing Intention

In some circles, setting one's intention has come to be accepted as the means for attracting the people and acquiring the things that we are convinced will make us happy. It is as if intention alone wills our every desire into manifestation. The question is, are we setting into motion a vision that represents our highest good? When we are willing to sit with ourselves long enough to understand the motivation behind our intention—whether it is to impress, satisfy the ego, expand consciousness, stimulate our will, or obtain our right livelihood—then our intention is empowered by this clarity.

When it comes to visioning, rather than using willpower, we express willingness. *Where there is willfulness there is a wall; where there is willingness there is a way.* Willingness is about being patient with ourselves during the visioning process until that "aha" moment when we realize, "That's it!

I've caught the vision." Don't be surprised if what's revealed through your willingness to get out of the way is greater than what you dared to imagine for yourself. When our intention to surrender is sincere, obstacles move aside and we come into attunement with our vision.

The Sacred "Yes" in Receptivity

Receptivity is an open, spacious mind and heart that tills the soil of consciousness into a fertile ground of "yes." It clears the way for deeper knowing below the surface mind, softening the hard-held places of cherished attachments and points of view that sabotage a more expansive perspective of the limitless possibilities for your life. When you are receptive, your consciousness becomes pliable, flexible, teachable, and this gives entry to new visions seeking to emerge in your life. It is like returning to our childlike innocence, open and receptive to limitless possibilities.

How Sweet the Surrender

Surrender is an expression of trust, a way of saying, "I am available to what wants to emerge through me. I give my consent to it." It is a recognition that we are cradled by Existence and are ultimately safe and secure, regardless of what enters our experience. Even during times of deep uncertainty, by not resisting the unique gifts it offers us we give ourselves the opportunity to realize that we are preparing to give birth to a deeper dimension of ourselves.

Surrender frees us from attachment because it is a declaration that we are willing to release from our experience the mental, emotional, and behavioral habit patterns that no longer serve us. It is a wider opening that invites into our awareness new insights, intuitive perceptions, expanded goals. Whether it's about surrendering to the God of your understanding, to the Higher Self within you, or simply to the integrity of Existence, the willingness to surrender whatever safety net you have created opens the way for your acceptance of and trust in what is revealed in the Life Visioning Process.

The Freedom in Discipline

Discipline is greatly misunderstood; it's been given a bad rap. Somehow self-discipline and self-control have become synonymous, which isn't accurate. Control involves the fearful ego that doesn't want its image tarnished so it outwardly expresses a particular set of protective behaviors; discipline applies discernment to the life choices we make and allows us to change direction in mid-course if required. Control is a form of mental bondage, whereas discipline is a form of freedom, which leads to another misunderstood word. Many think that freedom is a license to do anything they want to do, which can lead to destructive habits and addictions.

A disciplined mind is open to the influx of inner guidance and puts it into action. When it comes to our spiritual practices, discipline is the willingness to do what it takes to wake up because enlightened living is our priority in life. Discipline may take us beyond our comfort zone and require us to, as the late theologian and mystic Howard Thurman says, "give over the vital nerve center of consent" to develop in ways we previously resisted or hadn't considered. When applied to visioning, discipline is what keeps us in our seat when we want to look away or even run away from what is being revealed to us about us. Discipline ultimately becomes a "blissipline."

The Graciousness of Gratitude

Gratitude begins as a practice and in its mature expression becomes a way of life that is filled with the spirit of thanksgiving.

Since childhood, most of us have been schooled in the mechanics of gratitude, that it's good manners to say "thank you" even when we don't mean it. But genuine, spontaneous gratitude is much deeper. It is a feeling that arises when we realize the immense gift, the preciousness, that is Life. Getting in the gratitude groove softens the heart, opens the mind, causing even seemingly ordinary things to become sacred. We see and experience Life's magic. Gratitude is a prayer that acknowledges the gift of Existence, that we can laugh, dance, sing, love, eat, create, celebrate, heal, transform, and that we have been fully equipped to become self-realized beings. Gratitude opens our inner sight to the fact that we already have been provided all the gifts of Existence.

Embodying the five foundational qualities that support your visioning practice is made easier by incorporating simple practices into your daily routine. For example, when you awaken in the morning, instead of immediately running your day's agenda through your mind, pause, take a breath, and offer gratitude that you are on the planet another day to enjoy those who love you and whom you love. Before leaving for your workplace, even if just for a short period of time, discipline yourself to meditate, bless your day, and send out blessings to the world. On your way to taking the kids to school or performing other errands, surrender to what you encounter throughout the day by realizing it is all part of your spiritual practice—things like being patient with traffic and irritating drivers who also wish to arrive at their destination on time, long lines at the grocery store, and so on. Be willing to stop and assist someone by holding open a door, offering a smile. As you walk through the day's activities, instead of taking things and people for granted, be receptive to the hand of the grace easing the way for you through them. Place reminders of these practices on your bathroom mirror, refrigerator, calendar, in your car, on your desk. Get creative. Include your family members and make it fun. Everyone will benefit and you will realize how even the most mundane activities are rich material to work with and contain their own magic.

Chapter 2

The Four Stages of Evolutionary Growth

I'm ready to leap into what is real
I got a sweet invitation, a mandate of ecstasy
It's time to be free.

WHENEVER I'M TEACHING classes on the Four Stages and LVP, the inevitable question that someone asks is, "How did you evolve the Four Stages, and why just four?" Throughout this book you will find reminders that we are dealing with the limitless nature of being, which translates into potentially infinite stages of growth. For the purpose of working with the processes of the human mind, describing four specific stages of evolutionary growth offers LVP practitioners reference points to which they may return to ground their study and practice.

A Template for Inner Evolution

It was over twenty-seven years ago that I was a faculty member at the Ernest Holmes Institute teaching the universal principles of the New Thought–Ageless Wisdom tradition of spirituality. Students were eager to visualize their wants and desires without first visioning for a larger idea or purpose for their life. They didn't realize that visualization is a preconceived notion of what they wanted to have or happen in their life. This is understandable considering the popular saying that "if you can see it you can achieve it." The next chapters on the Four Stages will trace and qualify how want, desire, visioning, and intention-setting evolve into surrendering the outcome for the highest good of all concerned.

The Four Stages were created as a means of offering a template of the evolution of consciousness, as well as describing the mind-sets and behavioral patterns that must be cultivated and released in order to progress from stage to stage. Having a sense of what we have to look forward to whets our appetite to evolve. It's energizing and motivating to know that there is a way out of our limiting thoughts and constricting behavior patterns, that there is a much larger life waiting for us to just say "yes" and move toward. Having worked within the laboratory of my own consciousness as well as with many students and counseling clients, I realized that there is an inner impulsion within us that propels us in the direction of self-discovery. The Four Stages are meant to serve as outlines, not absolute maps, and each of us moves through them according to our own unique pattern of unfoldment.

The Faces of Authentic Freedom

"What does the word 'freedom' mean to you?" is a question I frequently ask students in my classes. Before I share their top four responses, you might be wondering what freedom has to do with the Four Stages of Evolutionary Growth and the Life Visioning Process. Ultimately, genuine spiritual practice is for the purpose of getting free from the limitations of the ego, including worry, fear, doubt, lack, and other neurotic causes of human suffering. To be alive is to desire, consciously or unconsciously, authentic freedom.

Sri Aurobindo, the great Hindu philosopher, describes the consciousness of a liberated being in this way: "The liberated individual who has realized the Self and Spirit within him, who has entered into the cosmic consciousness . . . acts by the light and energy of the Power within him working through his human instruments. This is a total liberation of soul, mind, heart, and action, a casting of them all into the sense of the cosmic Self and the Divine Reality." Life Visioning is an evolutionary technology that accelerates a realization of the Self and Spirit he describes, and the Four Stages reveal the areas in which we have yet to prepare our consciousness for that liberating realization.

And now here are the four most common responses individuals offer on the meaning of freedom: freedom of choice; freedom from restrictions imposed by outside sources, including religious, cultural, familial, and societal structures; freedom to do anything one pleases; and freedom from self-imposed limitations.

When exercising freedom of choice, the results will be determined by how aware we are of our full range of choices.

If we don't fully explore our choices, then real freedom will not be present in our choice-making. The freedom to do whatever we want to do is not genuine freedom, it is license. Getting free from what is imposed upon us by societal structures is an inside job, for even if we join a monastery we can't live completely outside of society's influence. Freeing ourselves from self-imposed limitations is informed by our level of psychological and spiritual maturity, which determines the methods we choose for this purpose.

Freedom is not license. When an individual is free it leads to what I call living a life of "spontaneous goodness," which is about not insisting that something happen, not manipulating circumstances so that they conform to one's desired outcome. You will learn more about the deeper aspects of surrender related to LVP in later chapters.

Through the application of faulty reasoning, individuals arrive at narrow, limited definitions of freedom. Others, through their spiritual awakening, have a more expansive realization and expression of freedom. Authentic freedom, they tell us, comes from a conscious realization of the innermost Self, because only the Self is free; it never has been nor ever shall be enslaved in any form. The Four Stages and LVP are vehicles that steer you in the direction of the freeborn Self.

Free, or Unfree?

No person or thing outside of yourself can make you free or unfree. Both are do-it-yourself enterprises. There is a paradox about freedom: all beings possess freedom of choice, yet few are actually free enough to choose. Most individuals do not make choices from a consciousness of genuine freedom. Instead, they are dictated by ego, psychological and emotional mind-sets, parental, religious, and societal conditioning. A choice to cling to desires, opinions, beliefs, and habit patterns that do not serve your evolutionary growth keeps you in bondage because it obscures awareness of the Self. On the other hand, when you choose to do the necessary inner work to reclaim your identity as a freeborn, individualized expression of Source, you will break the chains that bind you.

Freedom From versus Freedom For

There is a more evolved stage than freedom *from* something: it is freedom *for* something. It is the freedom to respond to our life purpose even when it isn't what our ego had planned for us. It is the freedom to create, to dance to the unique rhythm of our inner spirit. Living our potential to awaken, to self-express, to contribute our gifts, talents, skills as a beneficial presence on the planet fuels the heart of a free man, a free woman, a free being. When we gain our inner freedom we become contributors to the evolutionary thrust of the universe, to that which seeks to emerge in the human realm.

Action, not Reaction

Most people are not free; instead, they live in reaction to events of the past and present, as well as events they project into the future. We react because we have been conditioned to do so. If we don't begin to question our conditioning, our reactionary habit patterns will remain lifelong companions. When we choose to remain in ignorance we become a walking reaction to the circumstances in our life. We imagine that we are taking action when in truth we are in a mode of reaction. Reactions are unconscious patterns of behavior, be they directed at someone who pushes our buttons, something we hear on the news, the irresponsible driver who's texting in the car in front of us, or the grocery store that just ran out of our favorite veggie burger. Your willingness to get clear on where you stand in the reaction–action continuum within your life structures is the liberating key. The Four States of Evolutionary Growth will assist you in clarifying your position.

Reclaiming Your Birthright of Freedom
The truth is we were born free but we have forgotten! Layers of societal programming have clouded our capacity to recognize our Original Face and respond to the unique call of our inner voice. From the moment of our birth and throughout our formative years, we become dependent upon having all of our needs met from outside ourselves. As a result, it takes a certain amount of life experience infused with insight before we reverse the process and realize we must become self-reliant and tap into our inner resources in order to live a fulfilling, self-actualized life.

Freedom is our birthright, but what kind of freedom? The freedom of awakened awareness, which births wisdom-guided choices. *Choice is a function of awareness.* We wisely apply that functionality by expanding our awareness of our true nature, which is independent of outer circumstances, things, or people. It is about *being* something—our free-born Self. The paradox is that it takes some doing to get to authentic being!

The Four Pillars of Freedom

As we evolve through the Four Stages, we can see that there is an expanding sense of freedom experienced in each stage. The prerequisites for embodying the aspects of freedom within the stages are supported by four pillars: self-discipline, self-responsibility, self-awareness, and self-remembrance of your unique soul-expression. We must be disciplined in order to accept the responsibility that comes with authentic freedom. When we are self-disciplined, we tend to more consistently make wisdom-guided choices. Wisdom is a form of self-remembrance, for when we discipline ourselves to pause and turn within before we act, the Self reminds us to make choices that are in integrity with universal principles, to choose actions that anchor us in the ways of freedom.

In this very moment, on the spot where you now stand, you can choose to be free regardless of what has transpired in your life, regardless of what "they" have said and are still saying about you, regardless of your opinion of yourself, regardless of any external fact. Right now you can begin to identify the state of consciousness from where your choice-making occurs. Once you identify it you can shift it; you can expand it into mindful awareness.

Clear seeing emanates from your Essential Self, that place within you that has never been born and will never die. As Krishna taught his disciple Arjuna, "This self is never born nor does it ever perish; nor having come into this existence will it again cease to be. It is birthless, eternal, changeless, ever-same, unaffected by the usual processes associated with time. It is not slain when the body is killed" (*Bhagavad Gita,* chapter 2, verse 20). The Essential Self is a radiant ray of Source individualized into form as every man, woman, and child walking the planet. The delusory sense of separation from our Source, coupled with our conditioning, causes forgetfulness of our inherent freedom. The Four Stages of Evolutionary Growth and LVP quick-start our remembrance of that original state of being.

An Adventure in Consciousness

The Four Stages and LVP are reliable guides for your adventure in consciousness. A true adventure heightens awareness, because when we venture into new terrain our senses are on high alert and our consciousness is open, receptive, sensitive, and flexible. The efficacy of your work within the stages is dependent upon how willing you are to be honest with yourself. How open are you to questioning the answers you've come up with in order to create solid ground under your feet? I ask this because when introspecting on the first two stages, your ego may have to endure a few unexpected blows.

Although I have organized evolutionary growth into four stages, this doesn't mean it is a linear movement. (This is something you may have to remind yourself about as you study the stages.) Once you enter the process, you will notice that you are simultaneously working on various aspects within each of the Stages. The Four Stages are like taking an ultrasound of your consciousness so that you may identify where energy has coagulated or stagnated, created an inflated or deflated ego or a more evolved state of consciousness and expanded sense of freedom. They are a preparatory step in the Life Visioning Process, a time-tested method that hands you wings to soar into the liberating adventure of your soul.

Inner Work Involves Inspiration and Perspiration

Embarking on the journey to self-discovery involves your willingness to endure some perspiration as well as inspiration. Keeping your seat as you observe previously unknown aspects of yourself will call on qualities and capabilities that may be a new experience for you. Keep in mind that viewing yourself through the lens of the Four Stages is not for the purpose of categorizing your assets and liabilities. Rather, it is to objectively observe yourself with honesty and courage without judging what you see, to determine the next step in your growth, and to prepare the ground of consciousness for moving forward. If judgment arises, put down your gavel and gently bring yourself back to being the observer. Loving-kindness toward yourself is essential, along with not developing an attitude of inferiority or superiority (should you find yourself scoring highly in some aspects of the stages). The descriptions of each stage are simply a mirror for recognizing areas in which you have attained a certain level of self-mastery and those in which inner work remains to be done.

It is important to emphasize that in no way am I indicating that there are only four stages that lead to ultimate development, for certainly we must bend a knee before the Great Mystery that transcends all categorizations, forms, and practices. There are infinite stages of awareness that are beyond description. The Four Stages are a leaping-off point toward a grandeur of Reality that the human mind cannot wrap itself around. Spiritual practices taught by enlightened beings, saints, and sages in all spiritual traditions have been passed down to their students as expressions of great kindness and compassion with the caveat that they are simply maps to awakening. As is said, once the destination is reached, the map may be tossed away. True spiritual wisdom reminds us that the map is not the territory itself. We can't feel the wetness of water by looking at photographs of water; we must immerse ourselves in it. We can't feel the ecstasy of awakened awareness through reading about it; we must find it in our innermost Self.

The Four Stages of Evolutionary Growth

Stage One	Stage Two	Stage Three	Stage Four
To Me	**To It**	**Through Me**	**As Me**
Victim Consciousness	Manifester Consciousness	Channel Consciousness	Being Consciousness
In general, no transformative spiritual practice	Spiritual practices: affirmation and visualization	Spiritual practices: meditation, visioning, affirmative prayer	Meditation or any other spiritual practices are by choice
Victims believe their life is controlled by external sources rather than by self-choice or self-responsibility.	Manifesters make effective use of the law of manifestation and thus feel a sense of control over their life.	Channelers are aware of being a vehicle of the Spirit and live from this sense of ultimate surrender.	These self-realized beings sense their absolute Oneness with Source and have no sense of an egoic self.
"Why does this always happen to me?"	"I can use the law of manifestation to attract everything I want into my life."	"God expresses in, through, and as me." (small sense of separation)	"I am one with God." (no sense of separation)
The opportunity to give up blame and shame	The opportunity to give up control and a false sense of power	The opportunity to give up ego and a sense of separation	The opportunity to experience limitless awareness

Chapter 3

Stage One: Victim Consciousness

If I can let go the darkness will fade
If I can just let go
There's a light all around me
But the pain in my thought
Has kept me holding on
But I feel like letting go.

STAGE ONE IS CHARACTERIZED by a mind-set that "life is being done to *me* by *it.*" The "it" may be God, the devil, parents, DNA, a negative aspect in one's astrological chart, karma, the cosmic tumblers not rolling into place, or being born on the wrong side of the tracks. "Something outside of me controls my destiny" is the mantra of victimhood.

Victims frequently beseech an external deity to protect them from the hardship and suffering which they have imposed upon themselves. By excusing, rationalizing, or justifying their chosen behavior, they refuse to take self-responsibility and then plead and bargain to be rescued, often using words such as, "Dear God, I promise I'll never drink again if You just get me out of this mess."

Victims often live in a mind-set that people and life in general are out to get them. Their finger is always pointed outward rather than inward. Their stories become self-fulfilling prophecies which draw into their magnetic field people and circumstances that justify and solidify their victimhood. Victims are unconscious of how they harm themselves by refusing to take responsibility for their suffering.

Race Consciousness

Victims are easily swept up in the collective beliefs of humanity, also referred to as "race consciousness." Patterns of thought, beliefs, and behaviors within families, ancient and modern societies, religious groups, social clubs, and organizations contribute to the creation of the "collective mind." Examples include superstitious beliefs from as simple as "it's bad luck to let a black cat cross your path" to fear-mongering that leads to panic about cultures different than one's own, or that natural disasters are a "karmageddon" form of punishment upon Earth's sinful inhabitants. Who can forget the Y2K global panic, when all of our computers were supposed to crash, or the end-of-the-world prophecy for May 2011?

Compulsive Behaviors and Addictions

Victims have yet to develop self-awareness, self-responsibility, and self-discipline. The mechanisms of fear, ignorance, and lethargy keep them performing actions without questioning why they do what they do and how they do it. They live from reaction to reaction, from drama to drama, as in "I have drama, therefore I am," and complain to anyone who is willing to listen about what life is yet again inflicting upon them.

To armor against fears, worries, doubts, and other forms of mental and emotional pain, victims may resort to compulsive or addictive behaviors such as over- or under-eating, substance abuse, overspending, sex addiction, gambling, religious addiction, overworking, or other harmful behaviors. "My problems make me to do this. I have no other escape from my pain," they exclaim. With such a mind-set, it is challenging to enter the vibratory frequency required to access a larger vision through the Life Visioning Process.

The Cycle of Ceaseless Mentation

Throughout the day, victims mentate, which is to say that they regurgitate the same mental contents of yesterday, last week, a month, a year ago. It's a continual recycling of thoughts, inner conversations, and outer projections. Mentators are also candidates for emotional contagion. For example, when they read the newspaper they consider the doom-and-gloom headlines as validation of their mind-set that "life basically sucks." Then they call their friends and talk about the fears, doubts, worries, conspiracy theories, and tragedies occurring in the world without necessarily feeling compassion for the people who are affected by them; they simply need to fulfill their need to complain.

To remain in Victim Consciousness is to empower outside influences to dictate who you should be, what you should and should not do, and what your place is in life. Vital life energy that could be applied to creativity, joy, peace of mind, inner reflection, generosity of heart, spiritual growth, and independent thinking is siphoned off by the victim's lack of self-responsibility. Individuals in Stage One consciousness don't realize that they already possess all that is required to activate their co-creative powers, positively impact their life structures, and catch the vision of the next step in their evolutionary progress.

A sense of victimhood goes against our true nature. Fortunately, a person eventually grows weary of living in such a state of consciousness. "To hell with it," they say, "I just give up." Or, in the words of civil rights leader Fannie Lou Hamer, "I'm sick and tired of being sick and tired." This form of passive surrender creates an unexpected gap in the victim's mentation, causing them to ask, "What's this strange new feeling?" Once having posed the question, it simply won't go away. At first this is irritating, like an itch constantly demanding to be scratched. Then something else begins to occur: a growing realization that there just might be greater possibilities and a deeper purpose to life than previously thought. There is an opening to deeper inquiry, more availability to new ways of responding to life. Our challenges cannot be all about our bad bosses, life partners, children, neighbors, friends, and so on. We begin to ask new questions, such as "What can I do differently to live a happier, more fulfilling life?" As we take skillful action our relationships change—people respond rather than react to us. There is a new energy in our inner atmosphere, more spaciousness which reveals even more possibilities. People who avoided us move in closer, our children share more of themselves with us because they find us more appreciative of them. We rekindle our love life and our love of life.

Good News from the DNA Front

Victims frequently blame ancestral DNA and parental influence for their current life circumstances. There is no doubt that heritable DNA from our ancestral lines and the conditioning we receive from our familial environment have an impact on our development. As Darold Treffert, MD, professor of psychology at the University of Wisconsin, tells us, "We have generations of ancestral habits that created unconscious patterns for us to fall back on, embedding themselves in our DNA, if we let them. But in every second, every atom of every day, we have choices." Harvard University psychology professor Steven Pinker supports this view, saying, "We are only beginning to recognize that our genome contains information about our temperaments and abilities. Of course genes can't pull the levers of our behavior directly."

My friend Dr. Bruce Lipton was one of the first scientists to posit extracellular control. Conducting a series of experiments, he discovered that the outer layer of a cell is the organic equivalent of a computer chip and the cell's equivalent of a brain. His experiments examined in detail the processes by which cells receive information, and reveal that DNA is controlled by signals from outside the cell, including energetic messages emanating from our positive and negative thoughts, thus demonstrating that we are not victims of our genes. In his book *The Biology of Belief,* he writes, "I was exhilarated by the new realization that I could change the character of my life by changing my beliefs. I was instantly energized because I realized that there was a science-based path that would take me from my job as a perennial 'victim' to my new position as 'co-creator' of my destiny."

Also embedded in our DNA is our cosmic inheritance from Source as beings who are perfect, whole, and complete. Even though at this reading it may appear to you that you are separate from the wholeness of life, your Essential Self contains the holographic imprint of the infinite universe.

As science and spirituality converge, there is every reason to believe that discoveries such as those about our DNA and more will work their way from scientific, medical, psychological, and spiritual specialties into mainstream knowledge. This is the evolutionary impulse at play, propelling us toward that which seeks to emerge in, through, and as humanity.

The Mirror of Self-Reflection

Identifying the ways in which victimhood has a foothold in your consciousness is the path to breaking through and releasing them. The practice of self-reflection is a valuable mirror for revealing your conscious and unconscious patterns present in each of the Four Stages. If you are unfamiliar with introspection it may feel like a mental process; however, there is a more subtle energy movement taking place. To align with its flow, I suggest that you precede the upcoming Guided Self-Reflection with the following centering practice.

Centering Practice

Find a quiet place within your home where you may sit uninterrupted for about fifteen minutes. Take a posture of empowerment with your back straight, your feet flat on the floor (for chair sitters), and your hands upturned on your thighs in a position of receptivity. With either open or closed eyes, take a few long, slow, deep breaths. Relax into your body. Become aware of where you are holding any tension and breathe life energy into those places. If your mind wanders, mentally say "thinking" and simply bring your awareness back to the breath.

When you feel a sense of centeredness and readiness to begin the Guided Self-Reflection, in the language of your own heart affirm your commitment to the inner call of your true Self. You may use affirmative statements such as, "I declare my readiness and welcome this opportunity to become better self-acquainted for the purpose of my growth and development." Or, "I attune to my Higher Self. With grace and ease I intuit the next step in the higher vision for my life."

Guided Self-Reflection:
Identifying Victim Consciousness

As you participate in the following introspective practice, it is important to be honest yet gentle, which means dropping any judgment about what you observe. Take it as a work-play exercise and be sure to bring a sense of humor with you on your journey of self-discovery. You may wish to journal your observations.

- How do I relate to myself and my place in the world?

- Am I run by guilt and the need to appease an external deity?

- Do I blame God, others, or outside circumstances for my life situation?

- When challenged, do I react, or act?

- Am I living in a mental-emotional survival mode?

- Do I participate in compulsive or addictive behaviors? If so, what are they?

- What steps am I taking to get free from compulsive or addictive behaviors?

- Am I self-responsible?

- Am I willing to question my answers about who I am and why I have been born?

- Do I often ask, "Why me?"

- Am I often sidetracked by thoughts of fear, worry, doubt, lack?

- Do I give others responsibility for my happiness?

- Are there specific life structures in which I consider myself as either having been or currently am a victim?

- Does drama stimulate me and cause me to feel purposeful?

- Am I able to forgive myself and others?

How you respond to these questions is not the final answer. As you become more self-acquainted through the reflections and meditations at the end of each chapter on the Four Stages—and when you begin to practice Life Visioning—your answers will shift. *That you invest the time in your evolutionary progress is the pivotal point*, because it is an indicator that you are cultivating a sincere commitment to grow, develop, and become more aware when you are mentating. Thus, by doing so, you lay the foundation for creating a more expansive vision for your life.

Reflective practices are for the purpose of identifying those aspects within your life structures where your development is progressing and those areas in which work remains to be done. We all have places in our life from which we need to get unstuck, so there is no need for embarrassment or judgment. Observing our behavior patterns, identifying those we need to release and those we need to cultivate through inner awareness, leads to living a self-actualized life. Until we have a greater understanding of where we stand in the process, we cannot grow forward. Honest and courageous self-reflection provides the requisite awareness.

Moving Beyond Victim Consciousness

Moving out of victim consciousness requires taking self-responsibility. Self-responsibility can sound heavy, but a great lightness of heart comes when we are self-responsible. Break it down to response-ability, meaning we have the ability to respond to whatever arises in our experience. And when we do, we not only shift the situation, we shift our consciousness. When we react, we are coming from an old emotional trigger point, whereas when we respond we meet the situation freshly because new mind-sets and heart-sets are emerging.

Releasing Blame, Offering Forgiveness

Self-righteous blame is the undercurrent of victimhood. The stories victims tell always point to outside themselves for the root of the story they tell. These stories may, in fact, be historically accurate and offer evidence about why a person is convinced she can't move forward. In some cases, individuals draw attention or even fame to themselves through their story. Have you considered why television's so-called reality shows showcasing victims are so popular? (Think *Jerry Springer.*) Human beings have become voyeurs of victimization stories, as in the adage "misery loves company." Society supports victimhood by feeding right into our moaning and groaning about "what she said to me, what he did to me." In some cases it makes individuals feel superior, and in others justified in maintaining their victimhood.

One of the most potent actions supporting our evolutionary growth is giving our consent to releasing victim stories through acts of forgiveness. No matter how small or how great is a victimhood story, it is a profound practice to offer forgiveness each night before going to sleep so that you don't carry resentments into the freshness of the next new day. And this includes self-forgiveness.

Forgiving the Seemingly Unforgivable

The following is a tragic event that happened to a friend and colleague of mine, Azim Khamisa. He offers not only an enlightened message about forgiveness; he is a messenger qualified by experience in the extreme.

Fourteen-year-old Tony Hicks was angry that he lacked a father figure in his life and that his teenage mother knew nothing about being a parent. So he joined his neighborhood gang, where he found a sense of belonging and the perfect outlet for his anger over his life circumstances.

Tariq Khamisa, a student at San Diego State and the only son of Azim Khamisa, worked part-time delivering pizzas. One evening while making a delivery, as Tariq reached for the pizzas in the trunk of his car, he heard a strange sound behind him. Turning to investigate, he found himself staring directly into a gun barrel held at his face by Tony Hicks. "Give me the pizzas and your cash," Tony demanded. Tariq refused. The other gang members backing up Tony insisted that he pull the trigger. Tariq fell dead on the ground.

Tony Hicks was found by the police, scared and remorseful about his actions. The police phoned Azim and informed him that his son had been shot and killed, and that the murder suspect had been taken into custody. "It felt as if a nuclear bomb went off in my heart," Azim said. He plunged into profound grief. A Sufi Muslim, he had an active spiritual practice that he used to soften the rawness of his mourning, meditating as much as five hours a day to ease his broken heart. After a while, Azim was faced with the reality of having to move forward into the next step of his healing process.

Tony Hicks was convicted of first-degree murder and sentenced to life in prison at the age of fourteen. Eventually, compassion for the young perpetrator began to dissipate Azim's anger. As he put it, he began to build up his "forgiveness muscle," and through this realized that there were actually three victims involved: his son, his son's murderer, and the community at large. Azim requested a meeting with Ples Feliz, Tony Hicks's grandfather, who immediately told him that ever since that tragic day, Azim and his family had been in Ples's prayers.

Azim informed Ples about the nonprofit organization he founded dedicated to ending youth violence, the Tariq Khamisa Foundation (TKS). Ples gratefully accepted joining the foundation and today he and Azim travel across the country speaking at schools, recreation centers, and religious organizations. Millions of young people and their parents have benefited from their story. TKF has also collaborated with Discovery Education in developing a violence prevention program that has so far reached 10.5 million children. In 2005, Azim wrote a letter to California's governor asking him to commute Tony Hicks's sentence. Says Azim, "We humans continuously confront defining moments in our lives. Sometimes these events are joyous; sometimes they are tragedies. At these moments it's important to make the right choices. When we do, we are literally able to manifest a miracle and produce transformation in ourselves and others."

Azim's mission has drawn to him public appreciation from not only respected harbingers of compassion and forgiveness, including His Holiness the Dalai Lama and Thich Nhat Hanh, but everyday people who, through his programs, have been able to release the burdens of hatred, violence, blame, and unforgiveness.

Most of us will never face the extreme circumstance of Azim's loss of his son through a deliberate violent act. Yet in ways that we do find ourselves holding onto a victim mentality, we can benefit from Azim's example. As is made clear through the description of his inner process, forgiveness isn't about sentimentality or emotionality; it's about the challenging inner work of releasing a level of anger that the world in general supports. It's about rising above the status-quo mentality of "an eye for an eye and a tooth for a tooth."

Just as Azim's inner work began in the laboratory of his own consciousness by first forgiving himself for his anger, resentment, and thoughts of revenge, so must ours. We must reach down into our innermost core and discover

there our innate capacity to release blame, to release ourselves and others from any form of indebtedness, and begin
our forgiveness journey. The only thing there is to blame is
ignorance. Whether it's yourself or others who have fallen
or erred, it is a case of ignorance. Even if you think, "I'm
not so sure about that. I knew better but did it anyway,"
the fact that you weren't able to stop your action means a
certain level of ignorance was in operation.

Forgiveness Practices

The self-forgiveness practices that follow can be tailored to
your specific needs. You may want to write out or record
the suggestions below or those you customize so that you
don't have to memorize them. If you have to shout out
and keep shouting out your forgiveness statement until an
energy of sincerity infuses your words, you may want to
find a private place where only you can hear yourself.

Begin with the Centering Practice on page 45. Once
you feel quiet inside, identify something in your life for
which you haven't yet been able to fully forgive yourself.
Bring the details into sharp focus and allow yourself to feel
their sting, for by doing so you can shapeshift that energy,
in all of its magnitude, into forgiveness. Cradle yourself in
your heart and then silently or aloud speak words of forgiveness and release. For example: "I take responsibility for
my actions and forgive myself for all that I have knowingly
or unknowingly done to hurt myself and any other individuals. I release myself from the bondage of unforgiveness. I am

free, free in the freedom that has always been mine. I claim it now. Guilt, shame, and blame are now neutralized by the unconditional love, compassion, and forgiveness which saturate my awareness, my heart, my entire being. Right here and right now I am cleansed of the toxin of unforgiveness. I begin afresh and give thanks for this realization."

When it comes to forgiving others, you may want to consider taking a forgiveness inventory of individuals from whom you have withheld forgiveness throughout your life, or even as recently as yesterday. In preparation for the practices that follow, it is always helpful to begin with the Centering Practice.

Next, if it feels comfortable, visualize the person(s) you are forgiving and consciously direct the energy of forgiveness toward their image as you affirm: "I forgive you, (name or names), for knowingly or unknowingly hurting me. My forgiveness of you is total and complete. I am free and you are free. All is well between us."

In instances where you and another individual would benefit from mutually forgiving each other and the other person isn't available for some reason, you can still do your forgiveness work. The same applies to individuals who are no longer in the physical form. You may affirm, "I free myself and I free you from all blame of knowingly or unknowingly hurting me. Through the power of forgiveness all is well between our spirits. You are free and I am free."

Now, sometimes we don't at first feel authentic when affirming forgiveness. Maybe we just don't like the person who hurt us, or they don't like us. Remember that forgiveness does not give license to people to treat us as they please, nor does it have to mean that those who have hurt or abused us will re-enter our lives. *We are doing our inner work for ourselves, not for them.* We are making a statement that no one can determine or affect our destiny by their words, actions, or inactions. This isn't about making "nice-nice" through the use of syrupy words or high-consciousness language. Nor is it a denial or bypass of our pain—be it disappointment, betrayal, or whatever else. Rather, it is about being honest about our emotions while realizing that there are times when human beings—including ourselves—act out of ignorance.

The Art of Inquiry

The next tool to support you in moving beyond victim consciousness is the art of inquiry. I say it is an art because it is a fluid and creative means for opening a treasure trove of self-understanding and insight. Let's say, for example, that you are having a challenging experience at work that weighs heavily on your mind. For a few days you keep waking up throughout the night, which depletes your energy and reduces your resiliency. Finally, you decide to take dominion over the situation. First, you calm your mind through the Centering Practice. Your heart becomes softened and your consciousness is more open and receptive. In the next step you sensitize your intuition through inquiry, asking: "If this situation does not change, what quality must I embody for peace of mind?" Patiently, compassionately, listen with your inner ear of intuition. Whether you call it the universe, the Higher Self, or nothing at all, you will receive feedback about a quality seeking to emerge within and through you. When you shift your attention from resenting the painful circumstance to cultivating the emergent quality, your evolution is accelerated.

Our life direction is informed by the questions we ask. When we ask meaningful questions, the universe responds with meaningful answers. Something fresh emerges and we see a way out of what appeared to be no way. We transcend the externality of victimization and enter the interiority of transformation. Then our questions are asked from a deeper place within us. They have more substance, and through the answers we are given we begin to understand that our life purpose is to awaken, to evolve in consciousness, to become liberated. We draw to ourselves and joyfully begin to practice teachings that will usher us into the next level of our evolutionary growth.

Chapter 4

Stage Two: Manifester Consciousness

I was looking for fortune, searching hard for fame
'Cause I thought the money would ease my pain
Yes, I wanted a big car and a house by the ocean
I was getting nowhere it was wasted motion
'Til one day I realized to seek first the Kingdom
And all things and everything have been added unto me.

INDIVIDUALS IN STAGE TWO live from a conviction that things happen "to *it* by *me*." Their mind-set is empowered by an "I make it happen" application of the law of manifestation. A new understanding that thoughts directly impact life experience begins, in turn, to birth an awareness and appreciation of metaphysics, which is a description of a cosmology based on oneness, an organic whole governed by universal principles.

Before we get more deeply into the law of manifestation—or the law of attraction, as it is sometimes called—it bears repeating that we don't "graduate" from stage to stage in a linear fashion. Within our life structures we embody and express different qualities, in varying degrees, from each of the Four Stages, as well as overlaps and vacillations within them. Committed and repeated practice of the exercises in Stages One and Two clears out mental debris and the machinations of the great saboteur—egoic ignorance—thus preparing the ground for the practice of Life Visioning, which begins in Stage Three. Having said that, if you are tempted to jump ahead to Stage Three, I offer this caution: without weeding and tilling the soil of your awareness, your practice of LVP will not bloom into a lush garden of self-realization. Life Visioning is a consciousness-expanding practice that requires inner preparedness. Proper understanding of the law of manifestation and practicing forgiveness are preparatory tools.

What Manifesters Have Going for Them

Manifesters increasingly embody a sense of self-responsibility and accountability. They bring their thoughts and actions more into harmony with universal principles governing the universe, and through acts of forgiveness and making amends begin to heal and thrive within their relationships. A growing sense of inner spaciousness is felt as a result of releasing Stage One Victim Consciousness. Individuals begin to grow deeper roots into their true nature and cultivate what the Buddhists call *maitri*, friendship with oneself. The more deeply manifesters practice self-reflective exercises and the art of inquiry, the more they attune themselves to the next step in their individual unfoldment and are directed to spiritual teachers and teachings best suited to support them in their growth and development.

As the manifester becomes a more conscious participant in his/her life, there comes a tangible relief from the painful constrictions of Stage One. Embodying and living from the realization that they are co-creative beings with dominion over their life structures, manifesters begin to reap the benefits of self-empowered living. With a growing understanding that thoughts reproduce after their own kind, they begin setting intentions and activating them through visualization and affirmation. The term "metaphysics" enters their vocabulary.

The Metaphysical Law of Manifestation

Since the beginning of time, metaphysics has been present in many cultures. Aristotle, Plato, and Homer, as well as contemporary philosophers and scientists, have written and taught about the metaphysical laws governing the universe. The ancient Chinese and Egyptians, as well as the Incas, Aztecs, Celts, and others, taught and lived by metaphysical principles. According to *Funk & Wagnalls Standard College Dictionary*, metaphysics is "the branch of philosophy that investigates principles of reality transcending those of any particular science, traditionally including cosmology, ontology, and speculative philosophy."

Science has discovered that, at least on the quantum level, the placement of attention affects that upon which it is placed. Physicists Niels Bohr and Werner Heisenberg concluded that an electron exists only as a potential until it is measured or observed. If observation of the electron determines its existence, then it is a given that where an individual places attention/observation also affects that upon which it is placed. Thoughts are units of mental energy. Energy can never be created or destroyed; it simply *is*. Energy vibrates at varying frequencies, and the rate of energy contained in one's thoughts is the theory underlying the law of manifestation. The higher the vibratory rate of energy, the more potent is the thought. Thought-energy condenses into form, which is another way of saying that our thoughts contour our beliefs, perceptions, and convictions, which in turn inform the choices and actions that become our experiences within our fundamental life structures discussed in chapter 1.

Like a door opening to welcome limitless possibilities, through our thoughts we can invite in physical healing, prosperity, right livelihood, loving relationships, creativity, and spiritual awakening. When one has evolved from Victim Consciousness into Manifester Consciousness, thought-energy begins to be channeled in a mentally, emotionally, physically, and spiritually healthy direction. It is ours to touch, direct, and share at every moment.

It's important to point out that while placing our thought-energy upon manifesting a desired outcome does affect the result, thought alone is not the only causative factor in our life, any more than is karma. As such, that conclusion would be an oversimplification of the Great Mystery we call life. Whether a theory's root is scientific, metaphysical, mystical, nondualistic, theistic, or nontheistic, it's not the final answer. If we think we have all the answers that is a backward step: first, because we have become no longer teachable, and, second, because answers are revealed when we are qualified in consciousness to receive them. As the Buddha's metaphor so aptly put it, "My teachings are a finger pointing to the moon. Do not get caught in thinking that the finger is the moon." The laws governing the universe are not "the thing itself"; rather, they reflect the invisible lawfulness operating in the visible world. When we refer to First Cause, the Presence, Universal Law, it is our attempt to describe the nature of Reality. We are using abstract language about Reality with the awareness that we cannot describe it in mere words.

One should also keep in mind that when "bad things happen to good people" there is more to it than outer appearances. We cannot accurately judge the life circumstances of other individuals because we cannot see into the depths of their souls to understand why they experience life as they do.

To the degree that we can drop narrow, judgmental preoccupations and the need to hold to a specific belief so that we can maintain a sense of inner security—both of which limit our vision—to that degree we gain access to our inherent power of mind and its wise application. As many have proven, it is possible to manifest by activating our inherent co-creative qualities: an open and receptive mind, a loving and life-affirming attitude, a confident trust in the fundamental goodness of the universe and within our own Self, and a sense of Oneness with the unified field of existence.

Mastery, or Manipulation?

The manifester becomes highly energized when realizing that he has activated inner resources which previously sat dormant within him. Therefore, the importance of bringing a pure heart and a pure intention to consciously operating universal laws deserves emphasis. In Egypt, formally known by its indigenous African name, Kemet, when individuals were being initiated into greater understanding of these universal principles, they first had to prove that they were sufficiently evolved in consciousness to manifest not for self-aggrandizement or fulfilling desires for false power, but for living in alignment with the laws governing the universe. They achieved this through their example and how it impacted the community as a whole.

I know individuals who have used the law of manifestation to become what the world calls rich and successful. Not realizing that there's never enough of "more," they continue to manifest things without evolving in consciousness. In this way, manifesting can take on a false appearance of mastery. It can become a manipulatory technique that strengthens the ego's false pride in an "*I* manifest it all!" Although one's life appears to be outwardly improving, there is a potential pitfall: the manifester may become addicted to manifesting primarily in the external, material realm and thus postpone or even prevent self-realization found in the more advanced stages.

The "manifestation honeymoon" feels like it will never end. Self-satisfaction can set in to such a degree that it becomes enticing to build a condo and homestead in Manifester Consciousness. That is, until a new soul-whisper begins to once again cause that itching sensation, a signal that there is a yet deeper awareness waiting to be discovered. At this point, manifesters open to going beyond their newly discovered sense of seeming mastery over the outer circumstances of their life in favor of mastery of their *inner* life.

The Four Windows of Manifestation

When manifesters stop using the law of manifestation as a custom delivery service, windows of manifestation begin to open more widely. Manifesters then start examining assumptions about who they are and how the world works, their issues of entitlement, and where true happiness can be found. They understand that *there is a difference between what one "should be" and what one is meant to be. What one should be is input from outside authorities, and when it is achieved the ego says, "Look what I've done!" What one is meant to be comes from within via grace, which brings with it humility, surrender, and acceptance.*

Grace is the givingness of Source, which we tap into when visioning. Each of us is a unique configuration of

Source, and through your work in Stage Two, you are preparing yourself to catch what you are meant to be from the inner, grace-filled voice of intuition.

The manifester applies visualization, affirmations, and other spiritual practices to advance his or her evolutionary process. If one has an active prayer life, the tonality of prayer changes from beseeching an external deity to a more interior communion with the Presence. There is a growing sense of Oneness with Source and how it corresponds to its own nature within us. In other words, when we focus on its qualities of unconditional love, compassion, generosity, joy, bliss, peace, it corresponds to those same qualities which are inherently within each of us.

Before we begin looking into what I call the Four Windows of Manifestation, I'd like to share with you how they came into being. Although I'd been teaching them for many years, it wasn't until I sat on a panel on *The Oprah Winfrey Show* with several other individuals who were featured in the book and film *The Secret* that I realized the necessity of synthesizing them into a more formal structure.

It all began with an audience member who, with such a pained sincerity in her voice, asked, "Do tragic or bad things happen to people because of something they think? Are their thoughts actually to blame?" Additionally, for months following the program, I received literally hundreds of letters a week from individuals seeking answers to challenging situations in their lives. One woman wrote about her eleven-year-old daughter who had contracted leukemia, asking what either she or her daughter might have "thought" to bring this about. It broke my heart to think that as a parent she felt one or the other of them was to blame.

While it is natural for the human mind to seek answers to the life challenges we face, and although it is true that thought makes its impact, it is a great oversimplification that a mere thought causes earthshaking events, which we consider good or bad in our lives. The truth is far more complex and mysterious and, as mentioned earlier, depends greatly upon the vibrational potency of the thought. So the main point I made in response to both of these women is that we are never to blame the victim, including ourselves. While it's true that we are self-responsible for our life, nevertheless there are factors within the equation that transcend what the human mind can wrap itself around.

As you read through the Four Windows, I encourage you to journal about those places in your life where you feel an opening or where you want to expand your awareness into a deeper understanding of those places in which you wish to grow.

Window One: The Job Factor

The book of Job in the Christian Bible introduces us to a man who greatly suffers from calamity, loss, and disease. In Job 3:25, we see Job in predicaments to which we can relate: "For the thing which I greatly feared is come upon me, and that which I was afraid of is come unto me." The Job factor is a description of how individuals manifest that which they consciously or unconsciously most fear, resist, dread, worry about, and bring into manifestation by the constant, intense placement of their attention and observation.

When you place your attention upon fear, worry, doubt, or a sense of lack, the Job factor is set into motion. Turn-of-the-century psychologist William James wrote, "My experience is what I agree to attend to. Those items I notice shape my mind." To that I add that what doesn't get our *conscious* attention may nevertheless remain in our subconscious awareness and also impact our life.

The good news is that we can adjust Window One to let in thoughts that shift the energy frequency of negativity into to a higher vibratory rate of receptivity, self-discipline, trust, and confidence, because we realize that we are fully equipped to handle anything that life places before us.

Window Two: Lessons

The second window of manifestation gives entrance to lessons which draw to us people and experiences through which we grow, develop, and unfold. Even though we cannot see precisely *why* things happen, we begin to catch that we have a magnetic field into which we draw that which is in service to our expansion of consciousness. All of us can recall an incident which, when it took place, felt excruciatingly negative. Sometimes chronic problems may be an indication that we are trying to find inner happiness in an outer world we have created that is simply too small. Perhaps you prayed for some thing, some quality, some person to manifest in your life and then all hell broke loose.

This is a cleansing opportunity, even though it may not be obvious to the surface mind. From a larger perspective, this is a good thing because we are expanding our ability to handle life's disappointments and surprises such as divorce, job loss, and illness.

When contemplating lessons, consider this: there is a deeper dimension to your spirit that can create challenging experiences designed to propel you into manifesting your highest potential, to expressing the gifts, talents, and skills that you have come on the planet to deliver.

A major lesson I learned through Window Two took place over twenty-six years ago, at the beginning of my ministry, and is described in brief in the introduction to this book. For the purpose of this chapter, I will share a few more details.

Rumors began to spread at a church where, on several occasions, I had been a guest minister. Some members within the church encouraged me to candidate for the open position of senior minister, and I did so. Apparently, my application set off alarms causing some persons to spread gossip, including that I hadn't completed my final ministerial class and so wasn't awarded a ministerial credential. The most vicious remark, however, was from some members of the selection committee who were convinced that if an African American were made senior minister "it would bring down property values, and people would start parking on the lawn." They went on to describe more negative things about me in particular, and negative things about African Americans in general.

I immediately began practicing forgiveness toward those who hurled these racial epithets at me, even as I remained a candidate for the position. Soon after this event, I received an invitation to attend my first monthly ministerial meeting. The appointed day arrived and I was very enthusiastic about being among my colleagues.

As I neared the building where the meeting was being held, through an open window I could hear that a man had already begun addressing the gathering. When I recognized the voice as that of a highly respected icon within the community of ministers, I zeroed in on what he was saying. "There's something troubling happening," he nervously announced. "A young black man is a front-runner for the position as senior minister at one of our churches. This is a travesty, and we have to pray to prevent this from happening." Being the only black candidate within any of the organization's churches at the time, I realized he was talking about me! I was so stunned on a soul level that I froze in my tracks. I couldn't believe that what I'd heard came not only out of the mouth of this individual, but out of his *consciousness*. By the time I managed to get myself into the meeting room—and took a seat in the very front row—his tirade had stopped.

This experience, coupled with what was happening with the selection committee at the Orange County church, brought me to my knees, causing me to go beyond any concept of forgiveness I'd ever known. All I could do was surrender and let go of rancor, judgment, any residue of a desire to retaliate—all of it. The real inner spiritual work presented itself to me and I was able to reach that place within myself that revealed the true and pristine nature of these individuals. Genuine forgiveness and unconditional love bubbled up in my heart, enabling me to emerge from this experience free from blame or scars on my spirit. It became clear to me that I was not to pursue the senior minister position at the Orange County church, so I withdrew my application. Moreover, I realized that the time had come to dissolve my resistance to founding my own spiritual community: the Agape International Spiritual Center, which I founded in 1986.

I will always be grateful for this lesson of many years ago because it took me to a deeper level of commitment to the evolution of my own consciousness. And what I learned through it has served me well as the spiritual director of Agape's diverse community and the ancillary projects and programs in which I am privileged to participate.

Window Three: Blessings

At the Stage Two level, we begin to listen to the soul-whisper that life does not begin with birth, nor does it end with the dissolution of the body temple. There is a continuity of consciousness, an eternality to our beingness. This immortal aspect of our existence has been given many names including soul, Higher Self, Essential Self, *atman*, and takes on a bodily form of the dimension which it occupies at each point in our spirit's evolving journey.

You and others you know have had experiences you consider as having been uninvited, meaning you did not seek them out. However, quite possibly they occurred to support another individual in their evolution. This is why we cannot oversimplify and judge by appearances, because we cannot see the Great Mystery unfolding behind the scenes, which could be either a Job factor or a blessing in disguise.

Take, for example, a story in the book *The Wheel of Eternity* by Helen Greaves, which reveals how some individuals come on the planet for the sole purpose of being of benefit to other beings. Helen, a nun with clairvoyant abilities, was asked to help a grieving mother whose ten-year-old mentally retarded son had made his transition when he drowned in a swimming pool. When communicating with the boy's spirit, Helen understood that he was a highly advanced soul who had incarnated for the purpose of opening his mother's closed heart. When her heart had finally broken open and became filled with compassion, he ushered himself back to the unseen world through his seeming death. What appeared to be the tragedies of mental retardation and drowning were, in truth, vehicles of blessing to his mother. (This is not a denial of the fact that in the human experience we grieve the loss of loved ones. After all, the human form of our beloved ones becomes very dear to us, and rightly so.) At the close of every earthly incarnation we emerge as the immortal soul untouched by sickness, sorrow, or death.

Window Four: Collective Consciousness
Through the fourth window we view the collective mindsets of humankind. There are different "schools of consciousness" in which we find ourselves. Some individuals

are part of the collective mind that believes fear, worry, doubt, scarcity, lack, suffering, death, creationism, and a nature of sinfulness from which one needs to be saved are life's realities. Then there are those who are part of the collective mind who believe that bliss, enlightenment, primordial emptiness, immortality, wholeness, and oneness are the realities of existence.

It is impossible to interpret in human language Source, its creative matrix, and its relationship with creation. Descriptions such as the Absolute, First Cause, or Universal Mind are inadequate to convey the immensity of what we are attempting to describe. Lao-tzu was well aware of this and put it very succinctly: "The Tao that can be told is not the eternal Tao. The name that can be named is not the eternal Name." No matter with which collective mind-set we identify, the important thing to remember is that the Truth doesn't depend on our belief in it! It just keeps on being what It is.

Certainly there are more than four windows of manifestation. The four I have described are intended to provide just a clue so that we don't get trapped in the entry-level explanation of the law of manifestation by saying things to people like, "Oh, so what did you think that caused this situation to manifest in your life?" It is equally important for individuals who have made significant progress in the manifester stage to maintain a sense of compassion toward those who are beginning their walk into a higher understanding of the law of manifestation.

Guided Self-Reflection:
Identifying Manifester Consciousness

As in chapter 2, the following introspective practice is for the purpose of identifying those aspects of Manifester Consciousness present in your life structures. Consider it a work-play exercise, free of self-judgment and to be accompanied by a sense of humor. I suggest journaling your responses, especially if any of them hook your attention or trigger something within you—indicators that there is work to be done in that area, or that a deeper recognition of yourself has taken place. Many individuals have told me that they find it helpful to periodically revisit these questions—which of course is highly individual as far as how frequently to check back—answer them anew, and then compare those answers to their earlier responses as a gauge of their growth process.

Contemplate these questions:

- Do I trust myself with the responsibility for my life?

- In what life structures have I made conscious choices from a place of self-empowerment?

- Am I aware of the laws governing the universe?

- When I apply any of the laws governing the universe, do I do so only for personal gain, or do I include the good of others?

- Do I operate the laws with a sense of mastery yet surrender, or do I manipulate them with a self-centered agenda?

Stage Two: Manifester Consciousness

- Do I set intentions imbued with conviction?

- How would I rate my follow-through on my
  intentions?

- What is my motivation for applying metaphysical
  laws: to stabilize my life structures so that I may be
  free to focus on my inner growth; to expand my
  gifts, talents, and skills; to manifest acquisitions and
  accumulate riches?

- How do I relate and communicate with others who
  share with me their life challenges—do I have compassion, blame, or lovingly speak of self-responsibility?

- Where do I stand in relation to the Job factor?

- When it comes to my life's challenges, do I seek
  to understand what is beneath them and work to
  mature beyond limiting thought patterns?

- Am I conscious of the fact that I draw to myself the
  people, circumstances, and things that enter my
  magnetic field—invited and uninvited—because I
  place my attention on them?

- With which aspects of the collective consciousness,
  or collective mind, do I connect?

- Do I feel an inner Oneness with Source, or the God
  of my understanding?

Moving Beyond Manifester Consciousness

The cautionary instruction here is: don't get caught up in acquisition and accumulation. This is not where the journey of manifestation ends; it is an entry-level understanding that we live in a lawful universe and that through application of its laws we acquire factual evidence that we are co-creators of our life. As mentioned earlier, a pure heart and conscious intention equal skillful use of the laws governing the universe. One must also step out of egoic self-absorption and relate to giving as well as receiving, to sharing successes with others, to using the law not only for one's own benefit but for the world at large. Inflammation of the ego shrinks by devoting more time to practices such as self-reflection, inquiry, meditation, study with a spiritual teacher, and reading wisdom-filled books.

In moving beyond Stage Two, it is vital to understand the necessity of surrender. Not to an external, dominating, punitive, anthropomorphic deity, for of what use is free will if that were the case? To surrender is to yield to the next stage of your evolution. It is saying, "I'm available to what wants to evolve and emerge through me and I'm willing to practice and embody what that takes for it to do so."

The Tools of Manifestation

In Manifester Consciousness, we begin to detect how we limit our inner and outer life by having a shortsighted view of our true nature. Limitation is not an inherent quality; it is a conditioned belief. As Chogyam Trungpa Rinpoche wisely points out, "Only because we have innate wholesomeness in us can we feel the counterpart of that, the pain of discomfort, anxiety, and confusion." Limiting thoughts and beliefs that have been learned can be unlearned. Tools that are highly effective in restructuring our biology of belief in Stage Two are affirmation and visualization.

The Effectiveness of Affirmation

When making affirmations, we don't beg or manipulate something outside of ourselves to respond to our prayer; instead, we speak from that part of us that is inseparable from our Source. Affirmative statements activate the power within us to draw into our magnetic field that which we claim and affirm for ourselves, whether it's something required to stabilize our life structures, or to move into the next stage of our evolution. Affirmation also assists us in removing subconscious blockages that would hinder fulfillment of our affirmative declarations.

The importance of how conviction impacts the efficacy of affirmations cannot be overlooked. You cannot fool your subconscious mind, but you should not give up if at first you don't feel your words are imbued with absolute confidence that they will manifest. When you trustingly, patiently work with affirmations, conviction supplants doubt lodged in the subconscious, and attentive repetition anchors that which you are affirming.

The Power of Affirmation

Anyone interested in this book has no doubt heard about how neuroscience is making many advances in the study of the brain, revealing new insights into how neurons and chemicals combine to create messaging systems more complex than any technology invented to date. Public television once broadcast a documentary entitled *The Secret Life of the Brain,* which described, among other things, how the brain absorbs and integrates information. A student of mine told me about this as well as about her experiment of combining its principles with a class I was giving on affirmation. She learned that there are three lobes of the brain involved: one lobe which registers what one speaks, another what one hears, and the third lobe what one reads. So, after writing down her affirmation, she spoke it aloud a few times. Then she recorded and listened to it, and finally she read it silently. Prior to this experiment, she primarily affirmed silently. But once she compared her practice and the results of simply mentally repeating an affirmation, she realized that applying all three methods grew deeper roots into her consciousness and produced good results in her practice.

What follows is a step-by-step method for practicing affirmations which you can experiment with in the laboratory of your own consciousness.

1. Write down your affirmation, perhaps in your journal if you keep one. Make sure your affirmation is in the present, active tense, as in the example given following point 6.

2. Take a posture of potency, with your spine erect, feet flat on the floor, and relax—without slouching—the front of your chest in the heart area.

3. With either closed or open eyes, gently take a couple of deep, slow inhalations and exhalations.

4. Read your affirmation silently three times and enter the feeling tone within your words.

5. Record your affirmation and listen to it.

6. Speak your affirmation aloud, feeling the conviction in your voice. First speak it loudly, then more softly and slowly, until it becomes a whisper. Lastly, affirm it only mentally until you feel trust, confidence, and peace infusing your words. This will generate a sense that you already have what you are affirming rather than forcing something into being. Affirmation is a statement of power, not of force.

Let us say, for example, that you are seeking your right livelihood. Your affirmation may sound something like this: "I acknowledge the Love-Intelligence permeating the universe and living right within my own heart. In this moment I fully open to its wisdom and clarity, to the revelation of my right livelihood. I am open, receptive, and available to its intuitive guidance and catch it now. For this and so much more I give thanks."

The Power of Visualization
Andrew Newberg, MD, one of the founders of the new interdisciplinary field called neurotheology, the study of the biological basis of spirituality and mystical experiences, writes in his book *How God Changes Your Brain*: "Even if you

don't think you're good at visualization, your brain is built to envision virtually every thought it has. The more you visualize a specific goal in life, the easier it will be for you to bring that intention into your inner and outer reality." Today there is a great deal of information available on the practice and value of visualization. For the purposes of this book, I have kept to what is relevant to Stage Two consciousness.

Visualization uses creative imagination to see with the mind's eye the desired tangible or intangible object of desire. For example, it's now a common practice in professional sporting events for team members to see themselves making the touchdown, slamming the winning ball across the tennis net, making a hole-in-one on the golf course. Visualization is also used by students taking tests, where they see themselves answering all the questions with grace and ease, acing the test, and by those who desire physical healing. Others apply it by imagining themselves in the home of their dreams, having financial comfort, discovering their creative expression and right livelihood, building vibrant relationships, working with cancer and other physical challenges, and so on.

I remember an experience many years ago when I was coaching a basketball team. Most of the boys on the team came from families without a father in the household, and were experiencing poverty. I was the new coach on the block—along with my friend John—and we got the kids who didn't get chosen for any of the other teams. Now, I didn't know how to coach basketball; I'd never played except in pickup games. Undaunted, I decided to put visualization—along with rigorous practice—to the test on the basketball court. The coaches at the other schools didn't know our strategy, and I went from being pitied for having the "hard cases" on my team to being envied for winning the championship three years in a row!

On our team was a young man named Mark, the only one who came from a financially prosperous family. I wanted the team members to be exposed to other neighborhoods, so one day we drove Mark to his home in Beverly Hills. When we pulled up to the curb one of the guys asked, "What door is the one to your apartment?" "All of them," answered Mark, pointing to the entire home. "No, he means which door do you go in?"—his house had four entry doors—another team member attempted to clarify. Again, Mark repeated, "Whichever one I want." The team members only knew about apartments and became impatient with Mark because they thought he didn't want to point out which apartment was his. When he invited them inside, much to their surprise they realized that all the doors were part of one home and were not four separate apartment doors. Their imaginations couldn't stretch that far, which is why I had wanted them to see other areas of Los Angeles.

I share this to illustrate visualization's role in taking us beyond our current spectrum of imagination. The use of visualization awakens an interest within us to learn what lies beyond the borders of its limits. The answer is: Visioning.

Visualization and Visioning

It is vital to the practice of LVP to understand how visioning differs from visualization. Visualization utilizes the power of imagination; visioning utilizes the power of intuition. Visualization is a *doing* process activated by the imagination. It is an action because you are doing something, whether it's seeing the desired result in your mind's eye or creating a dream board with pictures of what you desire. Visioning is a *being* process achieved through an inner, direct perception of what is desired to be known from the subtler dimension of Reality.

The great Indian philosopher Sri Aurobindo provides solid support of imagination: "Imaginations that persist in the mind, like the idea of travel in the air, end often by self-fulfillment. Individual thought-formations can actualize themselves if there is sufficient strength in the formation of the mind that forms it. In fact, all imaginations represent possibilities."

During visualization you project into the Universal Creative Medium your desire for specific objects, conditions, or outcomes to manifest. You picture them, in great detail, in your mind's eye. For example, say that you aspire to be in a specific profession, say a movie set designer. A demonstration of these desires provides factual evidence that intangible thought-energy condenses into tangible form through a creative principle that can be consciously activated. Visioning, on the other hand, enables the practitioner to receive a direct impress upon consciousness through intuition. As Sri Aurobindo so aptly put it, "Imagination itself is in its nature a substitute for a truer consciousness's faculty of intuition."

Intuition is a direct knowing without the use of an intermediary. The Life Visioning Process provides the tools to access your intuition and apply it as a conscious act of co-creation.

✳ ✳ ✳

To summarize, you have now learned how the law of manifestation operates and how our application of it empowers us to be co-creators of our life experiences. Whether or not we are conscious of it, our thoughts, beliefs, and actions set this law into motion. Obviously, conscious application of this law is to our evolutionary advantage, so it is wise to integrate specific components in our spiritual practices that support our use of it, including affirmation, visualization, and, of course, visioning.

Your understanding of the Four Windows of Manifestation will support you in getting unstuck in Manifester Consciousness and instead making the highest use of this law.

Chapter 5

To Connect, Must We Disconnect?

Something is new about me.
I feel it with each breath.
There's a majesty about me.
I feel it in each step.

NOWADAYS, BEING "CONNECTED" means 24/7 availability. Emailing, texting, Twittering, calling, keeping one's website and Facebook status current seem essential to being and remaining relevant in the world. In addition to the positive impact of globally interconnecting humanity, the information era is also contributing to the creation of a high-tech, low-touch society. It is impacting language, the publishing world, education, and social revolts. Neurologists and other pundits, including Nicholas Carr in his *Atlantic* article, "Is Google Making Us Stupid?", point out the paradoxical downsides of not setting healthy boundaries or applying discipline to how we engage technology. Some have gone so far as to suggest that it is making us "spiritually stupid" by keeping us too distracted to participate in spiritual practices. But how about this: can using technology with mindfulness lead to beneficial social and spiritual connection?

As I pondered this question, I remembered something the Dalai Lama said and looked it up. It took less than a minute to learn that in May of last year he interacted directly with Chinese citizens, answering questions live on Twitter. According to the official website of the office of His Holiness the Dalai Lama, 1,558 Chinese people submitted 317 questions; 11,705 Chinese voted for the ten most important questions, and His Holiness responded to them in great depth. The session was a rare opportunity for the Dalai Lama to interact directly with Chinese citizens without the intervention of the Chinese government, definitely a valuable social and spiritual connection.

How about Thich Nhat Hanh? In 2008 he and his Plum Village International Sangha stepped beyond email lists and websites and began building a community on Twitter and Facebook. The motive wasn't simply to self-promote, build publicity, or crank out content, but to spread the message of mindfulness, how to awaken, and to begin a conversation with a younger audience not necessarily prone to organizational affiliation or traveling to Hanh's community in France. What they learned is that today's youth do desire spiritual connection and tools for awakening—obviously a beneficial spiritual connection.

A Time to Connect, a Time to Disconnect

As the founder and spiritual director of a Los Angeles-based 10,000-member spiritual community, with thousands beyond its walls who watch live video streaming of Agape's services and special events, visit our website, subscribe to our e-blast list, personally use Twitter and visit me on my Facebook site, I am keenly aware of technology's benefits and the challenges of not getting all caught up or over-whelmed. In fact, just recently Agape's website was down for over a week. At the same time I was having problems with my home computer and my cell phone had been mys-teriously displaced for a day. I had to laugh at myself when a slight sense of panic arose from a sense of being tech-nologically disconnected from the outside world. It was a good time to have cultivated the tools of an accomplished yogi: clairvoyance, telepathic communication, and biloca-tion. Not being quite there, I had no choice but to limit my communication to the household land line. It felt as passé as sending messages via carrier pigeon!

Not everyone uses today's communication technology with the mindfulness of the Dalai Lama or Thich Nhat Hanh, but it's definitely something to aspire to. They, along with many other spiritual teachers and practitioners, take the time to disconnect from all forms of social network-ing in order to connect to the "inner-net" through their spiritual practices. When we do the same, we have a more conscious relationship to the constantly occurring changes within our outer and inner environments, technological and otherwise.

Visioning: Connector of Change and Changelessness

When the great awakener we call "change" shows up in the inner and outer aspects of our life structures it can be overwhelming, even when it serves our growth and unfoldment. Just as we learn to adjust to the outer world's ever-changing technology, so must we learn to navigate the ever-evolving inner world of consciousness.

When the ego begins to recognize that it doesn't have control over change, we become unsure of our ground. That which is familiar begins to dissolve as we wait for the new to emerge. This is significant, because we begin to catch that there is an inner impulsion actively causing us to surrender the ego to the Self, the deeper aspect of our nature that is transforming us.

If you have applied yourself to practicing the exercises taught in Stage One and Stage Two, you have begun to appreciate the precious opportunity of becoming better self-acquainted. Through the Centering Practice, inquiry, self-reflection, affirmative prayer, and visualization, aspects within your life structures that require change have introduced themselves. With sufficient life experience, we come to the obvious conclusion that only change is changeless.

The practice of Life Visioning connects to the paradox of how change and changelessness combine to support transformation. Change is not mere "improvement." Improvement is outer, like when we redecorate a room in our home. Change is when we do a total remodel, transforming the environment from its bones to the surface. Likewise, we can improve a personality trait, such as using our will-power to become outwardly more patient, which is a beginning point. However, to literally transform impatience into patience is an inside job, because we are going to the bones of the inner cause of impatience and making the shift at the inner level which will manifest in our outer expression.

When we practice visioning, we connect to the change-less aspect of our ground of being, which intuitively informs us of what and how we are to shift in consciousness so that we may embody the next stage of our evolution. This is why one of the steps in the Life Visioning Process includes asking ourselves, "What qualities must I release in order to embody the vision?" What is it within us that literally "changes"? Our ground of being is the changeless soul, the individualized expression of our Source emerging as our individuality. In contrast, our personality is formed by the impresses upon us from family, society, education, religion, karmic tendencies—in other words, it is fashioned from outside sources *and therefore can be changed.*

The Value of Questioning

As we open more, the ego's protective barriers that keep awareness of our neuroses at a comfortable distance begin to crumble. Empowering questions help to create this opening and support us in unlearning what we've been taught to believe about ourselves. Discovering fresh truths about who and what we really are liberates us from thought-forms and actions that no longer serve us. By asking ourselves open questions, the mind becomes freer, more flexible, fearless, and more vulnerable and therefore ready for new adventures in consciousness. Asking questions indicates that we are willing to seek and receive intuitively guided answers, which is why there are visioning steps that include a questioning process, which you will do when you begin the practice of visioning in chapter 10.

Are You Watering Your Garden?

So often we come to the spiritual path motivated by inner discontent and the expectation that spiritual practice will replace it with happiness. Happiness does not have to be created; it is our true nature. The practice of visioning supports us in discovering happiness by revealing tendencies that sabotage getting directly in touch with the Essential Self where happiness, joy, and bliss reside. As we grow deeper roots into our inner riches, happiness becomes a way of life. As the teaching of the Hopi encourages, "Know your garden and where is your water," which is a way of encouraging us to become acquainted with the inner self and what nourishes it. Deconstructing the false self and uncovering the authentic self is an intimate process, and visioning will assist you with both. It will support you in identifying the "I AM" that you really are.

The Sweetness in Surrender

In order to move from Stage Two—where you have gained a degree of conscious control through use of the law of manifestation—you must now surrender control in order to move into Stage Three: Channel Consciousness. The challenge is that now that you finally feel in control,

control is the last thing you want to give up! With practice, you will notice that surrender occurs incrementally when you yield to what is trying to emerge. Be encouraged by knowing that you are releasing that which inhibits the next stage of your evolution and embracing what contributes to it. This is not an intellectual sitting-up exercise; it is a profound release of the ego's need to be in charge in order to assure your sense of maintaining a sense of a separate self. Ego is a hindrance; surrender is a freedom. Allow. Relax.

The butterfly does not contradict the caterpillar; it is a natural stage of its unfoldment. At some point the caterpillar surrenders to the impulse of transforming into a butterfly. When the evolutionary impulse begins to cause you to want to scratch its itch, you will know it. You don't have to feel anxious about surrendering to it. Allow it. Surrender is simply saying, "I am available to what seeks to emerge through and as me."

Taking the time each day to disconnect from the outer world and connect to our interiority through meditation and other spiritual practices brings us to a place where we can give a surrendered "yes" to life. This "yes" softens the heart and allows peace and trust to prevail.

Chapter 6

Stage Three: Channel Consciousness

So I say to myself, can this really be
Is this still small voice the way Spirit speaks to me
Touching me when I'm quiet, touching me when I'm alone
Opening me as I surrender to the way that's being shown.

STAGE THREE IS CHARACTERIZED by a "through me" state of consciousness wherein you become a clear, pure channel for the Essential Self and its qualities to freely flow. This description of Channel Consciousness can only fall short, however, because ordinary language is an imperfect tool for describing the numinous subtlety and intense rapture of consciously sensing the radiant energy of Existence flowing within one's being. The great

Sufi mystic Rumi awakens our own soul's longing for this realization through his poetry when he writes, "Your effulgence has lit a fire in my heart and you have made radiant for me the earth and sky. My arrow of love has arrived at the target and I am in the house of mercy and my heart is a place of prayer."

There are as many ways of realizing the union of Channel Consciousness as there are individuals, for each soul has its own unique romance with the Infinite.

Witnessing Your Excellence

There is an aspect of Stage Three awareness that can be compared to being "in the zone." Have you ever had an experience when it seemed like "something" took over and carried you to an unprecedented level? Maybe you were speaking passionately on a subject and found yourself saying things you didn't even know you knew; somehow the information was "just there." Or perhaps you were engaged in a physical activity, such as dancing, hiking, or playing a sport, when suddenly you witnessed yourself performing in a seamless, magical way. Athletes, poets, and artists alike describe such experiences, saying it's as though a heavenly muse transports them to a peak of excellence in their specialized field. Composers and musicians speak about becoming the music, and dancers describe how boundaries blur as they become one with the dance.

On occasions when you find yourself witnessing excellence, do you ever wonder why it has the power to bring tears to one's eyes? I believe it is because it strikes the chord of excellence within *us*. We become inspired to discover it within ourselves, to drop the inhibitions, prohibitions, and exhortations that interrupt the full flowering of our unique expression of excellence. Self-expression is so vital to self-actualization that it caused psychologist and humanistic philosopher Erich Fromm to say, "I feel that the only thing that will save civilization . . . is a renaissance of the spirit—a rebirth of the belief of man in himself, in his essential creativeness."

Our inner work in Stages One and Two scours and polishes the doors of our awareness, preparing us for a direct realization of the Cosmic Creative Principle alive within us. Creativity is the very pulse of our life. We cannot move, eat, make love, blink, or think without setting creative energy in motion. When we grasp that our thoughts and actions are energetic movements which create specific results, we understand what creativity is, how it is that we are capable of activating the law of manifestation, and why our very life is our art form.

When we fail to understand the true nature of our life's creative purpose, we experience a spiritual identity crisis. Life Visioning reveals to us our Original Face, the face we had before our parents were born, before societal conditioning made its impress upon us. Visioning provides a cosmic mirror in which we glimpse our true nature beyond outer appearances. As you open more and more to your innate creativity, you will recognize yourself as the vibrant life-artist that you are.

It's All in the Soul-Plumbing

I like to share this story about Asmar, a longtime friend with whom I shared soul adventures. The way Asmar shared his gifts and skills in the world was through his profession as a plumber.

Asmar once shared with me that the first thing he did when arriving at a client's home was to go under the house and meditate. Once in the meditative state, he began a conversation with the pipes, inviting them to tell him their story. Attuned to their communication, he intuited the plumbing problem and informed the client of the work to be done. However, he went beyond the call of duty, doing his job out of creative delight and love, and without charging the client for any extra work "communicated" after he had submitted his initial price. Before leaving a client's home, he blessed all those who lived in it, along with the house itself.

Within weeks of this writing about Asmar, he made his transition into a new dimension of life. Although I will miss him, I rejoice at how he lived his love of God and others full out, how he held back nothing in his giving-ness. He shall always be for me an example of the intuitive communication process practiced during Life Visioning, whether it involves livelihood, relationships, spiritual practice—again, all of our life structures. This is the crux of what it means to be a spiritual being having a human incarnation: to discover, accept, and express our inheritance of oneness with Source and channel its essence of excellence as we deliver our gifts, talents, and skills in the world. We cannot accomplish this simply by willing it to be so. Only by surrendering the ego's false sense of control and engaging in spiritual practice can we open ourselves to the full expression of Channel Consciousness.

The Role of the Superconscious Mind

In Stage Two you learned how to use the conscious mind for setting intentions in various aspects of your life structures and how the practice of affirmations, visualization, and applying the law of manifestation affects the demonstration of those intentions. In Stage Three, the conscious mind *does not participate in intention-setting*, per se. While you do set a conscious intention to skillfully participate in Stage Three practice, it is the superconscious mind that reveals to you the precise intention to set for the next stage of your evolutionary progress. In other words, it is the intuitive consciousness that reveals to you the highest vision for your life and how to manifest it.

The conscious mind is impacted by the chatter of subconscious self-doubt, worry, a sense of lack, etc. In contrast, the superconscious mind is unaffected by the conscious and subconscious and is reliant upon intuition. As Sri Aurobindo points out in *The Life Divine*, "The master-word of the conscious and subconscious is Life, the master-word of the superconsciousness is Light. In the superconscious . . . intuition manifests itself in its true nature."

To Do or Not to Do; To Be or Not to Be

In a society where doingness is more encouraged and awarded than beingness, it can be challenging to grasp that in "inaction" there is a great deal of "action" taking place. The slogan of the restless mind is: "Don't just sit there; do something"; the slogan of the tranquil mind is: "Don't just do something; sit there!"

Quite often, the first thing that happens when we give ourselves permission to sit and do nothing is that an avalanche of thoughts spreads mental graffiti across our mind, thoughts we'd rather avoid facing, which is one reason why we keep ourselves obsessively entertained and busy. We don't stay in our seat long enough for such thoughts to recede into the background so that we can feel the pulse of our own soul. When unwelcome and embarrassing thoughts begin to rudely intrude, an egoic voice masquerading as "inspiration" causes us to jump up and fulfill, at last, our self-promise to exercise, to clean the closet, or handle some other "urgent" activity—anything to escape acknowledging our fears, discontent, scatteredness, forgetfulness, boredom, unworthiness, anxiety—you get the idea. When you first sit to meditate, contemplate, or introspect, you bump into the seeming messiness of your life. See it as nothing more than an egoic intrusion and simply allow it to pass through. Don't bite the hook. Inwardly smile at the ego's attempt and install yourself as the ruler of your consciousness and move on.

Developing the ability to sit and "be" without a mental tug-of-war with "doing" is acquired through the consistent practice of meditation. As Osho aptly put it, "Meditation techniques are doings, because you are advised to do something. But in a deeper way they are not, because if you succeed in them, the doing disappears."

Perhaps you are already engaged in a meditation practice. If you feel it clicks with you, continue in it. Or, you may want to consider experimenting with the technique described later in this chapter. An interiorizing meditation method is best suited to preparing your consciousness for visioning. You will discover that even a ten-minute meditation prior to visioning contributes to potent results, and that a brief meditation period after visioning will support you in anchoring intuitive realizations received during your session. (A brief period of meditation is also recommended before and after the self-reflection exercises in Stages One and Two.)

Meditation: Vehicle of Stage Three Awareness

Although meditation was known and practiced in the West in the 1830s by the Transcendentalists, including Emerson, Thoreau, Whitman, Dickinson, and others, it found a strong foothold in the USA in the 1960s. Still, many non-meditators and cynics have the notion that it is self-indulgent. The truth is that meditation is *not* a selfish investment. On the contrary, when you begin to name the great mystics, idealists, activists, scientists, humanitarians, spiritual teachers, artists, inventors, entrepreneurs, and philosophers who have hugely impacted individuals, communities, countries, and our shared Earth, very often they credit a strong practice of interior prayer and/or meditation for inspiring their vision, mission, gifts, talents, and skills.

The medical world now recommends meditation as a legitimate contributor to healing. Dr. Andrew Newberg, MD, has published several books describing research results which indicate that meditation is associated with increased melatonin availability, which has anti-carcinogenic and immune-system-enhancing effects. The neurochemistry of meditation has also been shown to increase the production of serotonin, an important neurotransmitter and neuropeptide that influences mood and behavior in many ways. Newberg's studies on the neurochemical effects of meditation, coupled with established research on the neuroelectrical effects of meditation, indicate the profound and wide-ranging benefits and effectiveness that a regular practice of meditation offers for personal health.

It requires self-discipline to set aside time for meditation practice, to make it a daily priority in one's life. In our hyperactive society, it can be considered an act of spiritual chutzpah to turn off the cell phone, television, computer, and iPod to sit and seemingly do nothing. Experience has convinced me that meditation is the most powerful spiritual technology for discovering our fundamental, enlightened state of being, which is why I define it as "paying un-distractible attention to Reality." Contacting the Reality of your soul-essence in meditation sensitizes your ability to realize your Oneness with Source, to intuitively "see" your invisible soul-qualities, access them more easily, and express them in the visible world.

When you turn the searchlight of the five senses and the mind within, you won't find an accountant, actor, spiritual teacher, chef, wife, scientist, mother, father, friend, beloved—not even a spiritual seeker! Step beyond the thinking mind and you will liberate yourself from the accumulated identities under whose hypnotic spell you have been living. You are the Self, which has no name or label. Meditation blows back your hair and gives you a glimpse, perhaps for the very first time, of your Original Face, your true identity. From this vantage point you, too, will be one of those whose presence and open heart are blessings to all who cross your path.

Getting Started

Two essentials for practicing any meditation technique are sincerity of intention and surrender of the results of your efforts. By surrender it is meant that whether you label your meditation to have been good, so-so, or poor, you remain nonattached, nonjudgmental. Additionally, the results of your meditation don't always manifest during or immediately following meditation practice. You may receive an insight, feel a sense of overwhelming peace, or even agitation, long after your sitting, all of which are byproducts of meditation. The point is that we don't practice meditation simply to relax or become peaceful, although that will occur. Its purpose is not to strengthen our ability to use the laws governing the universe, yet this will happen. We also learn how to more patiently and skillfully weather challenging times, but neither is that meditation's goal. *The ultimate purpose of meditation is to awaken to your inherently enlightened consciousness.* You don't create enlightened consciousness; you find what already is and always has been there, just waiting to be discovered within you.

Sincerity of intention to wake up translates into including meditation in your daily routine, and earnestness about waking up means that you will be faithful to your daily practice of meditation regardless of how you feel, whether your meditation is going great or it's all over the place. Perhaps while engaged in sitting practice anger, fear, shame, insecurity, the agitation of a restless mind arise and you think, "What's the use, I'm getting nowhere! Obviously, meditation doesn't work—not for me anyway." The ego is results-oriented, and it will encourage you to stop whatever it feels it is failing at, hurling insults at your obvious ineptitude. Don't resist it; laugh at it!

Sometimes awareness is present and sometimes it is not. That doesn't mean anything is wrong with your practice. For a few moments you may be fully present and aware, and then the mind wanders. So what. Surrender the ego's need to "do it right." Surrender will deliver its own gifts, but it is senseless to predetermine what you think they are or should be.

Like visioning, meditation is not a progression from stage to stage; it is an evolutionary process that takes place within you, which makes it a valuable practice to apply within all four stages. In the beginning it appears more like an effort, because it involves some tension as you find a position that works for you, along with other details that eventually become as natural as breathing. Meditation is focused, yet playful. In other words, as we observe the antics and listen to the chatter of the "monkey mind," we don't get all caught up in thinking we're doing it wrong. As the Buddhists teach, we don't hold on too tightly or too loosely.

Identifying the Meditation Practice for You

When searching for a meditation practice, the one that best suits your nature and temperament will "click." It's important to point out that occasionally the mind endeavors to trick us into believing that, "Golf is my meditation," or "When I'm gardening I practice meditation." Once you have made sufficient advancement in your practice, you do develop the ability to carry the aftereffects of meditation into your activities. However, while you may be in a highly focused and/or uplifted state during an activity, it is not the same as what unfolds while you sit in the stillness of meditation with the purposefulness of awakening.

The portable aspect of meditation or mindfulness practice is that we can follow our breath no matter where we are, whether it's at the kitchen sink, on the golf course, working in the garden, or driving on the freeway. If you're stuck in traffic and begin to feel tense, you can follow your breath and calm down. In the midst of a conflict with a co-worker, you can place your attention on your breath and mellow out. None of these examples is meditation in its pure form; however, they are related to the breath awareness we practice in meditation.

Another device to be aware of is the commercialization of pseudo-meditation methods. You may have seen advertisements for machines promising that by using them you will "meditate like a Buddhist monk in just twenty minutes," or that by listening to a guided meditation you will be led into a transcendent state of consciousness. While these methods may produce some beneficial results, neither machines nor words can transport you into the soundless, wordless state of paying un-distractible attention to Reality.

My suggestion is to do your research on the various meditation techniques taught by reputable meditation teachers. When a method feels like it clicks with you, try it out for a while. If by practicing it you find yourself entering a deeper state of awareness, if you feel an inner affinity with it, go for it.

Location, Location, Location!

When first establishing a meditation practice, it is very helpful to meditate in the same location, because every meditation you have in the same spot builds up a vibration. Meditating consistently in a specific place magnetically pulls you back to sit. Just as when you walk into your kitchen it evokes a food, cooking, and eating consciousness, and your bedroom induces a relaxation and sleep consciousness, so does your meditation location amplify the meditative vibe.

Whether it's a room, a corner, or somewhere outdoors, your meditation space should be clean, uncluttered, and enhance a meditative atmosphere. Any phones, televisions, etc., should be turned off. You may also find it helpful to inform others who live with you that you don't want to be disturbed for the length of time you intend to meditate. If it's not possible for you to establish a specific location to meditate, that is not an excuse for not meditating. Wherever you sit, simply close your eyes and enter the sanctuary within your own soul.

Many individuals find it conducive to meditation to create an altar somewhere in their home and place on it devotional items related to their practice. Some persons like to light incense, chant, bow before their altar, and open with a formal prayer to remind themselves of their intention and as a gesture of respect for their practice. Regardless of how you begin your meditation, the practice itself should take up most of your sitting time. For example, you may pray and chant for five minutes, then meditate for twenty minutes.

While there is no specific meditation wardrobe, it is helpful to wear loose, comfortable clothing so that the body is not a distraction. Whether you sit on a floor cushion in the cross-legged position or in a chair with your feet flat on the floor, choose a position that suits your body type and physical condition. Arrange to meditate at the same time each day, both morning and evening, if possible.

As you become more advanced in your practice, noise and other distractions will not affect you as they do in the beginning—they simply blend into the background of your awareness and are no longer intrusive.

A Classic Meditation Practice

Although the *Shamatha* meditation technique described below is simple, in the beginning it will seem like an effort and "doing" will be present. If you are new to meditation, even a fifteen-minute sitting is sufficient to begin with. If you have had some experience, then begin with thirty minutes. Advanced practitioners may continue with their current length of practice.

1. Sit comfortably on a meditation cushion or a chair with your spine erect but without straining or overarching your back. If you are sitting on a floor meditation cushion, make sure your hips are elevated enough so that your back is not slumping and your knees rest flat on the cushion. Place your hands on your thighs, with your palms facing up or down.

2. If you wish, close your eyes. If not, lower your gaze and place it just about four feet in front of you. If closing your eyes causes you to feel sleepy, then it's best to practice with a lowered but open-eyed gaze. You need not focus on one spot, just rest your gaze. If sleep intrudes, reset your gaze a few feet more in front of you, or look straight ahead for a few seconds and then lower your gaze once again.

3. After settling into your posture, place your attention on the breath, which will be your primary point of attention. Begin by slowly taking two or three deep inhalations, remaining aware of the air as it enters and exits your nostrils. Then breathe in a natural rhythm. Since you may not be accustomed to observing your breath, at first there may

be a tendency to control the breath which may cause it to become irregular. Don't worry about this, as you will soon return to your normal breathing pattern. Just be with the breath as it happens, one breath at a time.

4.   Distractions such as thoughts, emotions, aches, and fantasies will arise, which is perfectly natural. Sometimes you will spin out for a while before realizing that your attention is no longer on the breath. Don't become annoyed with yourself ("Not again! When am I ever going to *really* meditate?"). Without frustration or judgment, mentally say "thinking," and with loving-kindness to yourself bring your awareness back to the breath. Even though you may be a seasoned meditator, each time you take your seat tell yourself, "This is the first time I am meditating." In this way you are not trying to recreate a meditation from the past or having a preconceived idea of what is "supposed" to happen.

5.   If at some point in your meditation a pleasurable melting into a sense of union with Source occurs, drop the technique and fully sink your awareness into this sweetness. When it subsides, return to your breath practice.

6.   Do something to signify the end of your sitting, whether it be reading an inspiring quote, a closing chant, a respectful bow, ringing a gong, or a

prayer in the language of your heart expressing gratitude to your teacher and the teachings you are practicing.

Things to Remember

- Visioning right after your meditation practice is ideal because your consciousness and heart are open and receptive, and your intuition is sensitized.

- There will be times when the effects of meditation will remain with you after you have left the cushion. It is possible to maintain these effects through mindfulness, which is another way of staying present in the now moment and performing activities with focus, precision, and awareness.

Ego: The Supreme Seducer

Ego, the great trickster, loves to mess with spiritual aspirants. So clever is this masquerader that it will do anything to hold you in its octopus grip, to prevent you from dropping your sense of a separate self. It utilizes false flattery and high-consciousness language to veil its gimmicks: "You sat for an hour. Now you're *really* making progress. I'm proud of you!" The farther advanced you are on the spiritual path, the more cleverly disguised and subtle are ego's encroachments. As proof we need look no further than to two of the world's most beloved examples: Jesus the Christ, and the Buddha.

One day Jesus followed an inner urging to go into the desert for forty days and forty nights to fast as a rite of purification. It's written that on one of those days he was standing on a high mountaintop, surveying the vast surrounding land and taking in its splendor. Seemingly out of nowhere he heard a voice promising, "All this I will give you, if you will fall down and worship me." It wasn't a case of fasting delirium caused by low blood sugar that made him hear Satan's allurement to become a real estate tycoon ruling "all the kingdoms of the world," as recorded in Matthew 4:9.

Twice more Jesus faced down the adversary of ego: once when he was tempted to satisfy his physical hunger by turning stones into bread, to which Jesus responded by saying that his spiritual discipline came before sensory satisfaction, and again when he was tempted to prove his spiritual powers by throwing himself from the pinnacle of a temple in Jerusalem. Ego cleverly advised Jesus that God would immediately send down a "band of angels" to catch him so that not even his foot would be pierced by a cobblestone on the street below. Jesus rose triumphant over all three seductions by not minimizing his vision, mission, or his relationship with God by satisfying the paltry ego.

Mara—found in Buddhist stories—is the lord of illusion created by the egoic mind and also resorts to similar tactics used by Satan. The Buddha, who was also fasting while he sat meditating under the Bodhi tree, was tempted by Mara to end his fast and preserve his physical health: "for there is only the slightest chance that you'll survive. My dear sir, do live!" Mara cunningly implored. Mara also appealed to the Buddha to abandon his spiritual mission, saying, "You could still lead the religious life, perform the offerings to the fire—a sure way to earn merit." Like Jesus, the Buddha's spiritual wakefulness reigned victorious over ego.

The obvious teaching from the example of the lives of Jesus and the Buddha is that we are not to live by the manipulations of the ego, which, as mentioned, become more subtle as one advances on the spiritual path. In Stage One Victim Consciousness the ego is consumed by "poor, pathetic me; look what they did to me." In Stage Two Manifester Consciousness the egoic mind-set of "I make it happen; therefore, I am the doer" rules. In Stage Three the ego says, "As a clear, pure channel of the Ineffable, all that I think and do is in alignment with the perfection of universal principle." Being alert to each stage's egoic shadow and checking in with ourselves keeps us aware of our motives for seeking to wake up. We don't become seduced into showing off any acquired *siddhis* (powers); instead, our joy is to live as a compassionate, loving, wise, grateful, humble, and beneficial presence on the planet.

Moving Beyond Stage Three

Applying the tool of meditation, the work in Stage Three is to dissolve the illusory separate self and instead to live from an awareness that the presence of God is expressing through you. In moving from Stage Three to Stage Four, this is to be realized: "My life is the very life of Source. There is no separation. Just as the wave cannot exist without the ocean, so do I not exist outside of my oceanic Source."

Stage Three: Channel Consciousness

As we progress to Stage Four Being Consciousness, we are accompanied and supported by all that we have practiced in the preceding stages. Stage Three literally represents the beginning of the Life Visioning Process in that you are learning, through meditation, to sensitize your faculties and become available to your superconscious intuitive awareness.

Chapter 7

Stage Four:
Being Consciousness

My heart is open, I am your instrument
Live as my life, shine through my countenance.

IT'S INTERESTING, IF not a bit ironic, that when it comes to describing the most advanced of the stages—Stage Four Being Consciousness—there is the least to say! It is a state of consciousness language can only fall short to define. Nevertheless, the world's spiritual traditions have considered it worthwhile to attempt defining the Ineffable and our relationship to it.

The line of demarcation between Channel Consciousness and Being Consciousness is thin, yet extraordinary. Stage Three channels Source "through me," while in Stage Four, Source expresses "as me." In Stage Three, effort is directed at dissolving the sense of being a separate self through meditation; in Stage Four, the practitioner has dissolved the egoic sense of self and continues meditating not out of necessity but for the joy of it, as well as to set an example for others. For those living in Being Consciousness there no longer remains a dividing line between oneself and other, oneself and other beings, oneself and Source. The living fire of Oneness has consumed any residue of separation.

The Desire That Satisfies All Desires

Stage Four is not easy to relate to and can even sound a little dry and unappealing from a human perspective, as in, "What? You mean I'll lose that great rush when I meet a goal? No more sense of achievement by the 'I'? Will I stop enjoying all the delightful pleasures of the five senses?"

Until we've had some taste of enlightenment, fulfilling our egoic desires seems like the ultimate experience, as successful Stage Two manifesters well know! When we finally own that 10,000-square-foot oceanfront home; when we get that hard-earned promotion; when we achieve the celebrity we seek; when we collect more credentials after our name; when we meet the person of our dreams—the "good life" will be ours at last.

It is natural to be partial to our own notions about what we believe contributes to our own personal good, how to achieve it, and what to do with it once it's ours. However, this becomes problematic when goals are achieved only at the material level. An emptiness remains because there is never enough of that which doesn't satisfy. In contrast, when a person living in Stage Three or Four consciousness acquires the same material things as someone living in Stage Two consciousness, their relationship to them is entirely different because they realize it has nothing to do with egoic motives or gains. They realize that absolute wealth is within, so their relationship to and handling of outer riches is with wisdom, nonattachment, and generous participation in the law of circulation. I stress this difference to avoid giving the impression that individuals living in Stage Three and Four consciousness don't acquire, appreciate, and enjoy all the adventures associated with embodied existence. They do. The point is that their motive does not come from egoic desiring, grasping, or clinging.

It is only when we realize our Oneness with Source that we can wholly appreciate the magic of creation's kaleidoscope, including the fullest enjoyments that the five senses have to offer, reaching our highest human potential, appreciating the beauties of the natural world, and playing our role full-out on the cosmic stage of life.

Glimpses into Being Consciousness

In chapter 6 we looked at how athletes performing in the zone enter an awareness of a Great Something overtaking them. They set out to compete depending upon their skill level, will-power, and rigorous practice when suddenly a greater power than they normally access becomes activated, taking them to a level of excellence expressing "through" them. You can see that in this Stage Three experience there still remains a sense of separation in that there is oneself *and* the mysterious Something which overtook them.

Some time ago I read a book by Bill Russell, former Boston Celtics Hall of Famer and one of the greatest basketball players of all time. In one chapter Bill describes an experience he had during a game wherein the instant he placed his foot on the basketball court he entered another dimension of awareness and knew where and when the ball was going to be passed. Ernie Banks, a former Chicago Cubs baseball player and a member of Agape, shared with me that he once went onto the field and knew exactly where the ball would be hit even before the pitcher pitched the ball.

In this state of omni-awareness, Bill and Ernie were more than *in* the zone, they were operating *as the zone itself*, a Stage Three or Four state of consciousness. To them there was no sense of an individual self *and* that which overtook them; there was only One Beingness. In the last analysis, in a state of Oneness there is no difference between the experiencer and the experience; they merge as one energetic essence.

Isn't it fascinating that there are instances where individuals who do not have a formal spiritual practice get a taste of Channel and/or Being Consciousness? An athlete, dancer, poet, musician, or artist may never have such a realization of Channel or Being Consciousness in any other life structure except their creative endeavor, and then only for fleeting seconds, moments, or a few hours. Then there are masters in the world's spiritual traditions who permanently reside in Being Consciousness, not only when in meditation or interior prayer, but throughout all of their life structures. Therein lies the Great Mystery beyond any of our philosophies, metaphysics, or mystical concepts. The Reality of existence is beyond any human constructs. Still, it is in our DNA to endeavor to plummet the depths of being, to learn what we are made of, to discover and live the limitlessness of our highest human and spiritual potential, and to unify with our Source. Even the human body is made of the stuff of stars. One of the world's leading cosmologists specializing in the formation and evolution of galaxies, Dr. Joel R. Primack, professor of physics and astrophysics at the University of California, Santa Cruz, described in an interview with *EnlightenNext* magazine how "All the heavy elements—carbon, oxygen, nitrogen, phosphorus, sulfur, iron, and all the way up to uranium—these are made in stars and in supernovae . . . That's what we are made of. We're the rarest stuff in the universe."

Stepping into Being Consciousness

There is a song in your secret soul that cannot be silenced. It sings its existential, unceasing melody within you. Then the day comes when, through your inner work, you hear and feel the vibration of its cosmic rhythm. Suddenly you unify with it in a realization of Oneness, of Being Consciousness. It may occur when you are in meditation, deep interior prayer, silent contemplation, or out in nature. There are no rules governing the time or place of its entry into your awareness.

There is a reason why mystics go into the forest, live in mountain caves or in the desert—why they seek seclusion to commune with God. In chapter 6, verse 10 of the Hindu *Bhagavad Gita* it is written: "Free from ever-hoping desires and from cravings for possessions, with the heart and mind controlled, retiring alone to a quiet place, the yogi should constantly try to unite with the soul." Now, you don't have to buy a ticket and head for the Himalayas in order to achieve enlightenment. But there is definitely something to say about deliberately allotting time—say, on a yearly retreat—for the sole purpose of leaving behind the clamor of the world and going into silence in order to devote more time to your meditation practice.

I'm reminded of a time when I visited my brother when he was a student at Sonoma State University. When I arrived, I decided to take a walk in the forest. I was so overcome by its majesty that I was inspired to sit and meditate. All at once I entered a state of Oneness with the trees, the air humming through the branches, the grasses, rocks, the birds—all of it. My clothing felt like a barrier between my body and the holy ground upon which I was sitting, so I took it all off and felt my body blend into Oneness with the leaves and earth. It was so transporting that it felt like the only reality of my life. Time evaporated as I embraced the spiritual elegance of the moment.

Just now, as I wrote that description, I recollected a time when I flew up north to give a talk. As I exited the plane and began walking down the ramp, I entered a mystical awareness of Oneness with all the other individuals walking down the ramp. Entering the baggage area, everyone standing there to collect their luggage became part of my expanded Self. When my ride met me I said to him, "This is amazing. I know all of these people." We stepped into the elevator and I wanted to hug everyone. They all felt like an extension of my beingness. It took a while to come back into my conscious mind, but for those few precious moments I sensed a much larger freedom, a grander reality. It was somewhat painful to forfeit that state of awareness, but through grace it left an indelible impress upon my consciousness.

Practice, Practice, Practice!

Source has given us the capacity to have an intimate at-Oneness with its Presence within ourselves and throughout creation. Cultivating and realizing that capacity is the ultimate purpose of our existence. Whether or not we accept that self-realization is achieved over lifetimes, in four stages or no stages, there is no doubt that it involves practice, practice, practice. Among self-realized beings who have left a legacy, be it written or verbal and recorded by disciples, each has clearly stated that ultimate states of consciousness require a spiritual practice, be it meditation, interior prayer, shamanic ritual, the trance of a whirling dervish—that which is beyond dogma, doctrines, theories, or theologies.

In addition to the knowledge that there are various levels or states of consciousness, it's equally important to understand the obstacles to the attainment of an enlightened consciousness. As you read the descriptions of the Four Stages, for example, your mind may be sizing up the level of your desire and ability to journey through them. Ego will cunningly advise you that in your current state of development you just may not have quite what it takes to participate in your evolutionary growth, so perhaps you should postpone it for a while. In this very moment, you can erase that self-doubt and any others that attempt to sidetrack you. Understand that the ego is heavily into self-preservation and doesn't want you to lose your attachment to it. What does it matter who or what you were before you arrived at the choice-point to wake up? No one and no thing can prevent you from realizing your true nature. That is, no one except yourself.

Meditation may appear to be one of the most challenging habits to form, especially since we have become such a speedy society accustomed to instant results. Your efforts may not be rewarded with instantaneous visions, seeing light, peace, joy, and so on. Meditative benefits may come slowly, but they will come surely. You don't have to take the word of self-realized beings when they say meditation will give you a certainty about your true nature; you can prove it for yourself. No blind faith is required. The results of meditation are real and come with practice.

There is a reason why in both Stages Three and Four the recommended practice is meditation. If you already have established a practice before beginning to study Life Visioning, or if you have just now undertaken a meditation practice, you know that it contributes to a deeper connection to your Essential Self and a growing desire to move more deeply into the spectrum of awakened consciousness.

Set an intention that as you evolve through the stages meditation will become your first and last appointment of the
day. When your spiritual practice is a priority, your mental
trend will keep turning you toward your practice. Even
after your sitting sessions you will notice how the aftaref-
fects of your meditation impact your activities, interactions,
relationships, choices—nothing remains untouched.

Let Us Meditate

Turn within with me right now for a guided meditation
on the truth that your individual consciousness has no
circumference, that it is unlimited and that you are absolutely qualified to realize your Oneness with Existence,
your Oneness with its unconditional love. Luxuriate in that
awareness for a moment. Breathe into it. Right on the spot
where you now sit, know that you are held on the lap of
omnipresent love permeating and upholding the cosmos,
beating in your own heart, flowing in your bloodstream,
thinking through your mind, walking in your feet, yearning to emerge through and as you.

Now bring to mind a moment or occasion when your
heart was on fire to know the truth, to discover your purpose of being. It doesn't matter whether your desire was
fueled by joy or by suffering. Fully enter the feeling tone
of that longing, that yearning to realize the Self. Take a
breath and amplify that feeling. Mentally say to yourself,
"I'm here to wake up. I'm here to have a realization of that
which is true about me, that which is changeless about

me, that which is eternal about me." Breathe life into that intention as you continue to focus on the breath. Realize that as you sit in meditation you are touching your eternality, your immortality. Contemplate the truth that you are an on-purpose, individualized expression of Source in form, that it wants to fully come into its own as you. Give your consent to a realization of your Oneness with the Spirit of Life. Relax into the Presence above and below you, to the left and to the right, in front, behind, and all around you. Feel and surrender into a sense of Oneness with that Totality.

After you have bathed your consciousness in this realization, give thanks for these precious moments spent in contemplative meditation.

I encourage you to practice the meditation instruction taught in chapter 6 on a regular basis. By doing so, you won't have to continuously refer back to the instructions because they will have become natural to you. Guided meditation is fine to include in your sitting sessions, but it is not a substitute for mindfulness meditation practice. Consider it an adjunct practice for integrating and embodying the essence of your true nature.

Out of the 7,093,965,809 (and counting) persons on the planet at this time, there is a small percentage who have as their priority a desire to awaken to their Essential Self. And out of the percentage who do meditate on a regular basis, arriving at the nondual state of Stage Four consciousness is a rarity. Even if you are reading this book and others that encourage you to evolve through a meditative practice, you are in the small percentage who have a karmic propensity to seek the desire beyond all desiring: self-realization. Now, that isn't a license to become a spiritual elitist or to cut back on your practice because you're practically "there." No. It is simply a way of encouraging you to stay on track and keep your spiritual practice as a priority in your life.

Visioning in Stage Four

When Stage Four Being Consciousness becomes our predominant state of awareness, we are living Spirit's highest vision of itself as us. We may still practice meditation and visioning, but not as a necessity. This stage of consciousness is not reserved for avatars and mystics. It is as much our inheritance as it is theirs. Liberated beings such as the Buddha, Jesus, Krishna, and other saintly individuals are not the great exceptions; they are the great examples who compassionately agree to grace the planet and contribute the gift of their awakened consciousness so that we, too, are shown the path to fulfillment of our divine destiny.

The Stageless Stage

In Stage Two Manifester Consciousness you learned about how difficult it is to give up the exhilarating sense of being in control, as in, "Finally I have dominion over my life and can attract all that I want to myself." It is even more challenging to move from a Stage Three awareness of "these are *your* hands, Spirit, use them; this is *your* mouth through which you speak; these are *your* eyes through which you see; this is *your* heart through which compassion pours"—into a Stage Four nondual consciousness of "Spirit as *me* doeth the work." It can, at first, feel impersonal, dry, lacking in that juicy ambrosia of devotion to the Cosmic Beloved. It feels like sacrificing the richest fruit of spiritual practice, which is why many mystics choose to remain in Stage Three rapture; it feels so certain that they have arrived at the highest pinnacle of ecstasy. Eventually, however, the hunger for complete freedom arises and the aspirant surrenders to the call of spiritual liberation.

Is there a stage of awareness beyond Stage Four? Certainly. The Absolute is in itself indefinable by reason, indescribable by speech. As Sri Aurobindo wrote, "The Absolute is the ineffable X overtopping, underlying, immanent and essential in all that we can call existence or non-existence. Before and after the beginning, now, forever and beyond Time is that which we cannot describe even as the One, even when we say that nothing but That is." Living, moving, and having your being in full realization of the Absolute as he describes it can be called the Stageless Stage.

Part Two

The Life Visioning
Process

Chapter 8

The Dark Night
of the Soul

*The world all around me was falling down
And when it crumbled I saw higher ground
Something happened inside of me
I stepped into my true identity.*

THROUGHOUT MY THIRTY-SOMETHING years
of teaching, it's been my experience that occasionally
individuals become disenchanted when I bring up "the
dark night of the soul." Sometimes this happens because
they have a preconceived notion that doing the spiritual
path "right" is about perpetual glee, which is a symptom
of spiritual immaturity. Yet, there are many times, in any
stage of consciousness, when the dark night overshadows
our desire to practice, grow, and transform. The mystics
and spiritual practitioners of any path will describe those

moments, days, months, or even years when divine succor is nowhere to be found.

Having experienced the dark night, I realize that its transformative impact should not be overlooked, under-estimated, or resisted. Its relationship to Life Visioning is also relevant. There are times, no matter how devoted and precise we are in our practice, when we cannot access our intuitive faculties because we are in the midst of an evolu-tionary shift in consciousness. Deep soul-work is occurring at a level we are unable to discern with the conscious mind, which can cause us confusion and frustration. Therefore, it supports our overall practice to understand that we are operating on many levels and stages of growth simultane-ously, which is something the human mind can't easily wrap itself around.

It's important to clarify that a dark night of the soul has nothing to do with the common definitions of psycho-logical depression, melancholy, despair, or sadness about life's challenging external circumstances, including tragedy or loss. (Certainly such events deserve self-compassion and have their life-changing value.) The significant difference between these experiences and the dark night of the soul is that such events affect our various life structures, whereas the dark night of the soul is a mystical process involving only the soul and Source.

A big part of misinterpreting the dark night arises from over-romanticizing the spiritual path, which occurs primarily in three ways: first, we believe only what we want to, for example that it is not our fate to feel soul-pain and we can avoid doing so if we pray, affirm, and think only in positive ways; second, if we meditate and perform enough good works as our teacher and his/her teachings instruct, we'll know bliss and be liberated in this lifetime; or third, getting caught up in religious emotionalism which is temporary at best, say from an inspiring talk or music, yet we don't have an interior spiritual practice to anchor and expand that inspiration, so we have to return again and again to get another inoculation from the external source of our high.

In the ebb and flow of practice, there naturally are those times when our prayers feel dry, soulless, and our twenty-minute meditation seems like an eternity filled with a litany of complaints, accusations, and criticisms, causing us to become confused and bereft of comfort. Suddenly, reading the headlines of a supermarket tabloid is far more alluring than the book we just bought on how to accelerate our evolutionary progress. A spiritual drought has set in, for how long we don't know, and it gives us grief. We may regress to old religious thought-forms and wonder if God or the devil is testing our spiritual mettle. Everything once considered real is now felt to be unreal, causing us to ask if the path we're on no longer serves us and it's time to once again explore the aisles of the spiritual supermarket. Whether we experience one or many of these symptoms, any one of them dramatically shifts our spiritual center of gravity. Ego can win these rounds, beating us down with self-loathing. Nevertheless, such setbacks in our spiritual practice still do not constitute a dark night of the soul.

Defining the Dark Night

I define the dark night this way: the dark night of the soul is a profound movement in consciousness that unravels the entanglements of ego, metaphorically bringing us to our knees by taking us through a seeming disintegration so that we may reintegrate at a higher level of consciousness. If we surrender and give our consent to it, we receive the dark night's gracious gifts. If we reject it, we miss its contribution to our evolutionary progress, for, as Jung points out, "The birth of the Self is always a defeat for the ego."

Many mystics in the world's spiritual traditions have written about their experiences of the dark night of the soul, including Saint John of the Cross, Saint Teresa of Avila, Kabir, Rumi, Hafiz, and others. If you read their life stories or poetry, you will note that their respective dark nights of the soul occurred in Stage Three awareness, with an overlap in Stage Four, and had nothing to do with external circumstances. Their intense agony was caused by the inability to access the Presence as they had become accustomed to do, echoing David's anguish in Psalm 51 when he cried out, "Do not take your Holy Spirit from me."

To the degree that one has an unbroken, intimate connection with Source, the more intense is the torment when the practitioner must continue the journey for an unknown length of time without the accompaniment of that blissful communion. However, upon emerging from the dark night they realize that they have been transformed, that incubating in seeming darkness and isolation transported them into a cleansing of consciousness, a greater dissolution of ego, preparing them for a more absolute awareness of Oneness. In the words of Saint John, "The divine touches the soul to renew it and to ripen it."

A Personal Existential Encounter

A number of years ago I found myself in the clutches of an existential dread so morbid I felt as though I wanted to die. I literally crawled to my meditation cushion feeling utterly disconnected from myself, God, and any sense of joy or happiness.

Once I managed to sit in meditation, what kept passing through my mind was every single mistake I'd made and the subsequent judgment I had placed on myself. Even something as small as inadvertently taking a pen from a hotel room escalated into a felony. Out of nowhere the ego's voice announced, "I don't want to be this spiritual!" This went on for most of the night, but it felt like eternity. You can imagine my relief when all at once a radiant light dispelled the darkness and I perceived myself the way God sees me—whole, luminous, as pristine as the moment I came into existence.

Although this experience involved a profound sense of separation, the reality is that there was not a moment when I was not embraced by the Presence. This taught me that by not resisting the dark night, it became a sacred doorway into a deeper confidence that we are, all along the way, escorted through our life by unconditional love, that light and shadow are not a duality but rather a dissolution of a limited perception of having a human incarnation. It also brought a healing understanding to a time when I had the constant companionship of the dark night for over two years. Even though I remained fully functional, an undercurrent of hollowness hounded my days. By the time I made peace with this and determined it would not sidetrack me from my spiritual practices, most unexpectedly I was filled with a profound sense of radiance and spaciousness. All of this made it clear to me why many of the mystics actually pray for a dark night of the soul experience.

You're in Good Company

As already emphasized, there is a tremendous difference between ordinary sadness and the dark night. The vibration is entirely different. Saint John of the Cross, a Carmelite monk from the sixteenth century, is perhaps the most sublime of all Spanish mystics. His book *Dark Night of the Soul*, a classic in mystical literature, is a valuable guide for navigating the dark night. In one stanza he writes, "O dark night, kindled in love with yearnings—oh happy chance! The endurance of this darkness is preparation for great light." His words reveal the dark and light aspects of incubating in the emptiness-fullness of it all.

When you're experiencing a dark night, I encourage you to read about the life of an awakened being and you will realize that you're in good company, for none have reached the shores of wakefulness without all of the ego's notions of what it means to be "spiritual" getting stripped away. Those who surrender, who don't resist the dark night, drop the remnants of ego and become a living fire of soul-luminosity.

While it seems more natural than unnatural to reject the dark night experience, you do so at the expense of a profound purification of consciousness. Let's say you are caught between two of the stages—your current state of consciousness and birthing into the next stage of your evolutionary progress—and you wonder if the benefits will outweigh the pain you are experiencing. A gauntlet is thrown down in the face of your ego, and how you respond is very revealing. Will you face it full on, as did Jesus and the Buddha during their respective dark night experiences?

So many individuals question why, when they're striving so diligently and everything has been going so well, there's suddenly "this" to contend with. After all, they've read all the right books, can talk the lingo, sit regularly on their meditation cushion, serve at their spiritual center. It's confounding, especially the first time it happens. Spiritual arrogance can be so subtle, but when we're sincere in our spiritual walk we remain humble enough to admit that no matter how long or how deeply we've traveled the path, we still know very little. This I call "positive ignorance," because it demonstrates an open and teachable attitude which acknowledges that there remains a distance to go on the journey to enlightenment.

Don't Avoid the Void

"Don't avoid the void," I like to say and often remind myself. Sit with it. Don't try to affirm it away. Welcome it, without morbidity or a sense of victimhood. Remind yourself of this good news: often, right before you have a breakthrough you have a breakdown, a releasing, a chemi-calization that becomes an alchemicalization. When you come through it, transformation has happened.

As you spiritually mature you will recognize that there are different levels to the dark night. They will become easier to surrender to because you will learn to recognize and appreciate their cleansing effects.

Navigating the Dark Night

When experiencing a dark night of the soul, I've always leaned into theologian Dr. Howard Thurman's wise advice to walk in "remembered radiance." When we recall the communion we realized in deep interior prayer, or a pre-cious meditative Oneness with the Whole, we gather the courage and surrender to keep on keeping on. It is a way of metaphorically holding our hand in loving-kindness and remembrance that moments of darkness always lead to the Light. When we mature in our understanding of the valu-able play of light and shadow in our life, we know that we are on a grand journey of the heart and we give thanks to the dark night for evolving us into spiritual warriors and illuminating our path. You may welcome the dark night with full confidence and trust.

Chapter 9

Preparing the Ground of Consciousness

I've heard your voice before
Your way has been calling me
Now I'm walking through the open door
I'm ready to listen now.

NOW THAT YOU have familiarized yourself with the Four Stages, it's time to go more in depth on the vital role they play in visioning. Although intuition has been introduced throughout the book, it will become both more subtle and overt as you sensitize yourself to the breadth of its role in all aspects of your life structures. While visioning's beauty lies in its simplicity, if a practitioner has not previously made conscious contact with their faculty of intuition, it will take a little time and practice to attune yourself to knowing when you have tapped into it. More than likely, you have used intuition on many occasions without having given it a name. Intuition is a powerful touchstone, and as you practice visioning more and more you will realize how often it has guided your decision-making throughout your life. Any time you have said to yourself, "Oh! Why didn't I listen?", you don't usually follow up with, "Listen to *what*?" because there is that within you that knows you are referring to that still, small voice which later says, "I told you so!" This illustrates how available our intuition is, how it is always ready to provide input when we are ready to listen.

Right where you are—in whatever mind-set or heartset you find yourself while reading this sentence—is the perfect launching point for your practice of Life Visioning. "Uh, are you sure? I mean you don't know how I . . . (fill in the blank)," you might be saying. Granted, after reading about Stages Three and Four in the previous chapters you may feel incarnations away from living in a "through me" or "as me'" consciousness. The truth is that unless we are highly illumined we can't know precisely where we stand in our lifetimes of evolutionary progress.

What I mean by that statement is this: from a superconscious soul-level you may have chosen to work on a specific aspect of your development in this lifetime. Once in the human form, however, the conscious mind tends not to recollect such soul-decisions. Unless you are sufficiently evolved to have absolute knowledge of the entire chain of your past existences, you simply can't know how far or how close you are to liberation from the wheel of human birth and death. As Paramahansa Yogananda wrote in *The Divine Romance*, "To know firsthand about reincarnation [your previous lives] you would have to have a continuity of consciousness during the transition period of death, the afterdeath state, and the prenatal state in the mother's womb, from one incarnation to the next. It is possible." Highly evolved individuals bring with them an awareness of their incarnational purpose and at a young age find the spiritual practice to support it.

Regardless of how you relate to your evolutionary progress, it's always good to remind yourself that growth and development are not linear, which translates into the fact that we may be highly evolved in some aspects of our beingness while having a distance to go in others. This can become humorously awkward if, say, the ego regards itself as quite intellectually evolved yet trips all over itself when trying to fit into ordinary social situations where accumulated knowledge isn't the entry ticket.

We may have just a glimmer of our true nature, a moderate recognition, or a deep realization of who and what we are and where we are going. There's no race to the finish line; we all evolve according to our own unique pattern of unfoldment and, although it can be accelerated, it cannot be forced. Whether we believe we live one life or many lives is not that important. The point is, how are we going attune to the next step in our evolutionary progress in *this* lifetime? That is both the question and answer to which we make ourselves available in Life Visioning.

A Brief Retrospective

It may have been a while since you read the earlier chapters on the first two stages, so a brief overview may be in order. In Stage One Victim Consciousness individuals live from a mind-set that a power outside themselves is running their life and is to blame for the circumstances in which they find themselves. By cultivating a sense of self-responsibility, self-awareness, and the activation of their co-creative powers, forgiveness, and the art of inquiry, they begin to break free from the stranglehold of victimhood.

Individuals living from a Stage Two Manifester Consciousness have discovered the law of manifestation and realize that their thoughts directly impact their life circumstances. Their sense of self-empowerment and self-responsibility have matured, and they enthusiastically enter the world of metaphysics. To move beyond Stage Two, manifesters learn to surrender the ego and not merely manifest on the external level; they also learn to grow deeper roots into their inner being through affirmation, self-reflection, and other spiritual practices.

Stage Three individuals live in a "through me" awareness of the Essential Self and its relationship to Source, while Stage Four persons live in an "as me" state of Oneness with Source. Although visioning is more fully orbed in Stages Three and Four, it is also highly useful when applied to Stage One and Two aspects within our life structures, and in the following chapter you will read about individuals who have done so. Because the intention of this chapter is to prepare the ground of consciousness for visioning, we will now explore what is essential to its practice.

Visioning Isn't Visualization

As mentioned before, it is vital to the practice of LVP to understand how visioning differs from visualization. Visualization utilizes the power of imagination; visioning utilizes the power of intuition. Whether it's seeing the desired outcome in your mind's eye or creating a dream board collage depicting that which you desire, visualization is a *doing* process activated by the imagination. Visioning is a *knowing* and *being* process arrived at by an inner, direct, intuitive realization.

During visualization you project into the Universal Creative Field your desire for specific objects, conditions, or outcomes to manifest. Manifesting these desires provides factual evidence that intangible thought-energy condenses into tangible form through a creative law that can be consciously activated. Visioning, on the other hand, enables the practitioner to receive a direct impress upon consciousness through intuition. Once again, as Sri Aurobindo so aptly put it, *"Imagination itself is in its nature a substitute for a truer consciousness's faculty of intuition."*

Hunches, Instinct, and Intuition

"I knew it!" is our response to an uninvited hunch about how something would turn out. These are times when for some unknown reason we get an urge to have our tires checked only to find a four-inch nail in one of them. Or we instinctively decide, against all contrary logic, not to drive thirty miles to attend a concert for which we bought expensive box seats and later learn it got rained out. These hunches and instincts are cousins of our uncultivated faculty of intuition. Although people often use these terms interchangeably, they are not synonymous. A hunch or an instinct is a hint, but *direct knowing is only possible through intuition.* Imagine the mistakes in judgments, presumptions, investments, marriage, profession—in all of our life structures—that we could avoid by cultivating our intuitive faculty.

It should be kept in mind that we cannot *force* intuition to happen. However, there is much we can do to cultivate our intuitive resources. Visioning is one such practice, because it "allows" rather than forces. It is based upon inner surrender, which creates space for intuition's voice to be heard.

Where Do You Stand?

Now is the time to pause and examine your present concepts and use of intuition. You may want to journal your responses to the following questions so that you can track your progress in cultivating and applying the tool of intuition throughout your practice of visioning.

- What is my current understanding of intuition?

- What hunches, premonitions, and instincts did I catch but did or didn't act upon?

- How has intuition played a role in my life?

- Do I consider intuition practical and useful?

- Do I rely upon someone or something outside of myself for guidance—spiritual readers, medical, or other intuitives? Under what conditions?

- Do I consider my own intuition reliable?

- Am I willing to cultivate my intuitive resources?

The Visioneer's Window

Believe it or not, our intuitive faculty has access to more information than Wikipedia and is probably more accurate! There is no desired information or knowledge, quite literally, that fully developed intuition cannot access. *Intuition is a direct knowing without the use of an intermediary.* Intuition provides us with that which we did not gather through education, books, or personal experience. It is a direct tapping into Universal Mind, a non-reliance on any external source of data. "Intuitive thinking is perception-like, rapid, effortless," notes Princeton University psychologist Daniel Kahneman. In contrast, he adds, "deliberate thinking is reasoning-like, critical, and analytic."

Many indigenous cultures consider intuition as natural a faculty as the five senses, referring to it as the sixth sense. Everything that they do to support their individual lives and that of the village is informed by their intuitive connection to Existence. Their rituals of vision quests, tribal councils, chanting, dancing, and dreaming connect them directly to the intuitive realm. In the West we scoff at such actions, relying instead on meetings, conventions, summits, and boardroom rational logic to solve the challenges of organizations and of the world. We rely on many sources outside ourselves for our mental, emotional, physical, and spiritual well-being, when we ourselves have the capacity to use and trust our own intuitive guidance. I'm not, of course, discounting Western rationale, which has its place; I'm saying that there is a more reliable alternative.

Through the practice of Life Visioning, visioneers open the window of superconscious intuition and discover directly from their core being the purpose of their existence and how to express it through the vehicle of their life structures.

Intuition goes beyond dependency on the five senses and the conscious mind for the formation of ideas, values, decision-making, and principles by which to live. Through activation of the intuitive faculty a very specific type of integration begins to take place, synchronizing and harmonizing our physical, mental, emotional, and spiritual beingness. A new sense of truth-hearing, truth-seeing, truth-tasting, truth-smelling, and truth-touching occurs. Spiritual sight is activated within the heart, a spiritual energy infiltrates feelings and a transforming light breaks through the limitations of ordinary thinking while a new power of inspiration, intelligence, perception, and realization are activated in the mind and consciousness.

Human beings are the only life forms on the planet that are *consciously* innovative, creative, and can choose to evolve in consciousness. The mind is a potent faculty, and when it is opened to its fullest potential and informed by intuition, new realms of thought and action are accessed, making it possible for us to receive direct influences from higher dimensions of Reality. This Great Knowing within us causes us to say, "This must emerge *through me*," and so inventions, innovations, and artistic creations consistently appear on the planet. You catch the Divine Ideation that has been waiting for you to cultivate the favorable inner conditions so that it can express itself in, through, and as your life. Visioning prepares your consciousness to become that condition. So why not consciously attune yourself to that intuitive voice which cannot fail you?

The Interactive Components of Life Visioning

Life Visioning is based on the principle that all that exists emerges from Divine Ideation, by its cosmic thought-energy condensing into form. As individualized reflections of our Source, we also work with the cosmic energy inherent within our co-creative nature and express it through our various life structures. If that sounds a little nebulous or on the dry side, consider the cosmic undercurrent of all creation and the first component of visioning: unconditional love. I mention this now because the primary atmosphere for the practice of visioning is a feeling tone of this incomparable love.

Love is the fundamental truth of Spirit's being, the energy of its powers. It is directly from our Source that the capacity to give and receive love as parent, child, friend, and lover has been implanted in our hearts. As Sri Aurobindo puts it, "Love creates a unification of being, a power and joy and intimacy and closeness of soul to soul, of the One to the One."

Love is not merely about sentimentality, which is influenced by human emotion and attachment. Ordinary love may feed the ego, whereas unconditional love strengthens the heart and soul. Unconditional, divine love is the givingness of Spirit present within every atom of creation. Having chosen human beings to be vehicles of this love indicates how Spirit loves and respects us. There is no condition or behavior that would cause this love to be withdrawn from us. When we totally open and receive this unconditional love because we realize we are worthy of it, it will be a day of great blessing for us because then we will begin seeing life clearly and expressing love in their true nature. This is why love is the first interactive component of Life Visioning: We are so loved and trusted that we have been given the capacity to freely co-create our individual life with Source.

The second interactive component in visioning is deep listening. While this skill is within everyone, most people don't use it during everyday conversation, let alone for attuning themselves to the intuitive guidance available within. Deep listening involves reverent alertness, being wholeheartedly present, whether it be listening to another person or to the inner Self.

We prepare for the deep listening required in visioning through meditation, the third interactive component, whereby we attune ourselves to the finer vibratory voice of intuition. Our physical ears can hear only certain rates of vibratory sound. Intuition reveals the reality below the sounds of the physical and mental worlds.

Deep listening is the heartbeat of meditation. As we become more and more attuned to it, our ear of intuition becomes sensitized and we build trust in our intuitive faculty. The art of listening attentively to the soul's voice becomes a joy to us.

Your absorption and practice of all that has been presented in this chapter is a powerful inner preparation for your practice of visioning in the next chapter.

Chapter 10

The Art and Science of Visioning

The power of God is guiding me to
surrender to what I've got to be
With God all things are possible
With God all things are bountiful.

THE LIFE VISIONING PROCESS is a transformational technology that changes lives. The art of visioning places us at the helm of this co-creative process, and the science of visioning enables us to activate it through the laws governing the universe.

There is a continuity to our individual chain of existence whose length and breadth reaches from Earth to Infinity. Each link is forged by the choices we make, the vastness of which is both mind-boggling and awe-inspiring. The point is to choose and act from a consciousness that supports our life purpose and accelerates our evolutionary growth. Visioning has been designed to do just that by setting creative action into play within our life structures.

Now you will begin your visioning practice. I suggest you read through the material first, then set aside a block of time to practice. Allocate at least fifteen to twenty minutes to meditate prior to visioning. You may want to turn off your cell phone and any other sounds that may be a distraction. Have your journal at your side, and prepare to enter the sanctuary within and be introduced to your Self.

Visioning and Intention-Setting

The tendency seems to be that individuals set intentions without first having a clear vision. This is a backwards approach. Why invest the time and energy it takes to set intentions when they may not be aligned with your life purpose? Wouldn't it be wiser to *first intuit your vision and then set your intentions in support of it?*

An ideal order for intention-setting is first to meditate, then vision, and from a place of wisdom-guided intuition set intentions for how you will take action on what has been revealed to you. You will also benefit by journaling as a way of keeping your intentions before your inner awareness.

On Fulfilling Your Vision

Fulfilling your vision is greatly dependent upon your willingness to both cultivate and release the qualities which are revealed to you during the questioning segment of your visioning session. Throughout our lives we have been criticized as well as praised by various authority figures. This causes a formation of strongly-held notions about what constitutes our positive and negative traits. Therefore, you may be surprised if these qualities don't come up when visioning in steps 3, 4, and 5. Of course they may, but qualities you have given little thought to or have no awareness of will also be revealed. The point is to avoid as much as possible projecting your own or others' judgments about yourself into visioning. This will maintain an unbiased, clear, and open field of receptivity. A skillful means for accomplishing this is to develop the quality of nonattachment.

How Attachment, Detachment, and Nonattachment Affect Visioning

Have you ever considered how attachment holds you hostage to habitual patterns? One of the greatest gifts you can give yourself is to gently, compassionately work on releasing attachments. Perhaps you may fear that by letting go of attachments your life will take on a dull shade of beige. There's no need for concern, because nonattachment doesn't mean giving up your precious morning ritual of drinking organic green tea or moving from a palatial home into a cave just for the sake of being "nonattached." As the Buddhists teach, if one's only possession is a begging bowl it is just as easy to become attached to it as to a palace. *What nonattachment means is letting go of clinging to cherished desires, opinions, beliefs, and thought and behavior patterns that are the cause of unskillful habits, compulsions, and neuroses.*

In order to better understand the interplay of attachment, detachment, nonattachment, and the Life Visioning Process, let's first examine attachment and detachment. Attachment is an exaggerated attraction we have toward people, situations, environments, possessions, and our own projections about "how it ought to be." Also included are our mind-sets of justification, rationalization, and the inner armor we've built around our heart to protect us from hurt. When we are attached to a particular defense mechanism, for example, we fear letting it go because we become vulnerable, which causes us to feel exposed, unsafe, and insecure. When the habit of being defensive arises in our interactions with others, we tend to defend even our defensiveness.

Attachment to a desired outcome constricts and limits the results of our visioning practice. We are prevented from catching the highest possible revelation because it is sabotaged by our clinging to how *we* want it to be due to our conscious or unconscious attachments. Nonattachment is playing full-out, with all systems go, without attachment to the outcome. Detachment is saying, "I'm not going to play any more because I don't want to be hurt or suffer loss." It often leads to withdrawal, to disengaging from a person who has hurt us, from a workplace where we feel taken for granted, from any form of threat to the ego. It is a state of seeming indifference, sort of a "the hell with it" attitude accented by "I don't care anyway!"

Attachment and detachment operate in Stages One and Two consciousness by showing up as stubbornness and unwillingness to stop wallowing in victimhood or releasing the attachment to being a manifester. However, as we continue to check in with ourselves with unflinching honesty, we can begin to break our agreements with attachment and detachment.

Nonattachment is inherent within Stages Three and Four consciousness because self-love, a sense of interconnectedness to all beings, and Oneness with Source co-exist within those stages. While detachment and attachment push us away from love, nonattachment takes us toward love. It is an affirmative self-relating to our true Essence, our highest potentiality. Now, that doesn't mean that we're no longer challenged by traces of attachment or detachment, for as I have consistently emphasized, the stages are not linear, so states of consciousness do fluctuate and overlap, especially during an occurrence of the dark night of the soul. Our evolutionary process is fluid, not static, so we can expect to shift back and forth, in and out of the stages.

When it comes to visioning, nonattachment allows us to be fully open and receptive to what is revealed. If our visioning reveals that more sessions are required to fully download intuitive guidance, we are grateful for such an insight and remain trustingly patient. If we are guided to see that we must first cultivate or release certain qualities in order to fully live our vision, we find within us the surrender, willingness, and commitment to do so. If we have a potent visioning session, we are thankful without getting all caught up in having "done it right." We are nonattached to the results and are simply grateful for all that has been revealed.

To gain more than a superficial understanding of nonattachment requires further in-depth study than what is described here. Many of its aspects can be quite subtle in relation to the inner workings of our individual psychological and emotional traits, along with what our spiritual practices are. Any effort you invest toward learning more about the benefits of nonattachment will enhance your self-contemplation, visioning practice, and life structures.

A Way of Seeing

The following exercise has been designed to support you in becoming aware of where you stand in relation to attachment and nonattachment and how they interfere or empower the results of your visioning sessions. By increasing your focus on what you record in the right column, watch how what is in the left column begins to fade away. Exercises such as this contribute to setting a solid foundation for visioning. You may want to journal your responses and check in now and then to note your progress.

Habits, beliefs, opinions, and actions to which I am attached that inhibit my ability to open to what is revealed during LVP:	*Mind-sets and heart-sets that support my ability to be open, receptive, and nonattached to what is revealed during LVP:*
1)_____	1)_____
2)_____	2)_____

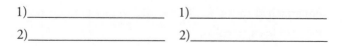

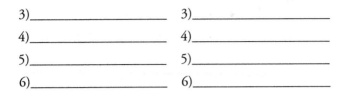

3)_____   3)_____

4)_____   4)_____

5)_____   5)_____

6)_____   6)_____

The Seven Steps of the Life Visioning Process

A note to the wise practitioner: don't be fooled by the seeming simplicity of LVP. Its potency is in the *depth* of entering a meditative state of consciousness and activating the intuitive faculty.

In service to practicality, the seven steps of LVP are given in the order they are to be practiced, followed by a more detailed description of each step.

1. Find a quiet location and, for least fifteen minutes, meditate to calm your thoughts, sensitize your awareness, and activate your intuitive faculty. As you observe your breath entering and leaving your nostrils, focus on opening and softening the heart. (It may be helpful to reread the meditation practice described in chapter 6.) Feel deeply into your heart and open to its atmosphere of unconditional love.

2. Keep in mind that Absolute Love is not the relative, romantic love or sentimentality. It is a total love given without a sense that it has to be earned through some meritorious act. It is love for the sake of who you are, just as you are. Sense this love

filling the entire atmosphere around you. When you feel you have reached a state of openness and receptivity, silently or verbally affirm your readiness to enter the Life Visioning Process.

3.   Next, mentally place your question before the intuitive faculty of the Higher Self: "What is the highest vision for my life? What seeks to emerge in, through, and as my life?" (Or, in the case of a project or business: What is the highest vision for this project or for this business?) Listen with reverential alertness, as though the greatest mystery of the universe is about to be whispered in your ear.

4.   When you feel ready, move to the next question. Ask: "What must I become in order to manifest this vision? What qualities must I cultivate?" Without censorship or judgment, open to what comes through.

5.   Ask: "What must I release to manifest this vision?" (This may include habits, mind-sets, compulsive behaviors—things of that nature.)

6.   Ask: "What talents, gifts, skills, and qualities do I already possess that will serve this vision?" (This moves you into a state of being and having, rather than trying to "get" something.)

7.   In the language of your own heart, no matter how completely or incompletely the vision came

through, give a sacred "yes" to it with full trust that more shall be revealed.

8. Enter a state of gratitude, knowing that the vision is already taking form, that it has been vibrating within your being since you came into existence and that you are now ready to allow it full expression in, through, and as you. (This "yes" is your willingness to be and do what is necessary to allow the vision to manifest.)

It's All in the Details

Now we will take each of the seven steps and fill in the details, which will provide a fuller understanding of why you are doing what you are doing.

Step 1

By opening and softening the heart center, you make yourself receptive to the omnipresent, unconditional love infusing your being, a love that infiltrates the cosmos and greets you everywhere you go. (You may find it helpful to remember a time when you felt loved unconditionally by a parent, grandparent, lover, or friend who loved you just for who you are, not because there was an expectation or need you fulfilled for them.)

Beginning your visioning session with meditation is the doorway into an intimate at-Oneness with the Source and its intuitive whispers in your secret soul. In this step you are giving your consent to hear the inaudible and see the invisible.

With each meditative breath you are giving your body temple permission to relax and to release any tension or anxiety, which paves the way for you to dive into the deeper dimensions of wisdom, knowledge, and intelligence that are already yours.

Step 2

Posing questions to Universal Intelligence bends your knee before its omniscience and omnipresence, its Love-Beauty. It is an expression of humility, a declaration that you realize there is a difference between your plans for yourself and the spiritual ideation of what is your true calling and the highest vision for your life. This loosens the tendency to project preconceived preferences into the Life Visioning Process, which oftentimes is what we think we should be rather than what we are meant to be. *What we "should" be is pumped into us from outside sources. What we are meant to be is already living at our center and is what we are seeking to discover through the Visioning Process.*

When you are in a state of receptivity you make yourself available to what is beyond your current capacity to imagine for yourself. This is important to grasp, because sometimes we have resistance to what is revealed. "No, that vision is too big for me. I don't really want to do that. That doesn't sound like me. It's outside my self-concept." If you don't resist, judge, or criticize yourself for such thoughts and continue with your visioning sessions, your resistance will wear itself out.

As in step 1, you are training your consciousness to become receptive to the feeling tone of deep listening with the inner ear and seeing with the inner eye of intuition.

Whether you call it your Oversoul, Higher Self, Great Spirit, God, or no name at all, this Great Something is constantly broadcasting its unconditional love and support to all beings. Ultimately, the revelation of the vision that is seeking to emerge through you will come in a form you will understand, whether as a feeling tone, an image, a sound, a meaningful symbol, or an intuitive insight. As you deepen your visioning practice, you will develop the skill to accurately interpret the responses you receive.

Individuals ask how long they should remain in this stage before moving on, especially when they don't receive a response. If nothing comes into your awareness, you may need to reach deeper within by meditating longer. Or, because the process is new to you, it may take a while to acclimate yourself or to settle down the mind. There is no reason to be discouraged. Simply remain in the silence as long as is comfortable and return to your practice at regular intervals. It helps to remember that a vision is not caught by force; it comes through surrender.

Step 3
By asking what qualities you must cultivate in support of your vision, you come into direct contact with your growing edge. We cannot receive what we are not willing to become in consciousness, so by asking, "What must I become, how must I expand my consciousness?" you begin to consciously transform. The more you are committed to your evolutionary progress, the more you are willing to take action on the responses you receive.

The truth is that within our core Self we already know what we must become to live our vision, yet because we humans have a tendency to fear change, we avoid or silence this inner voice. After all, we can't predict the overall effect it will have on our life structures. We may lose friends, mates, jobs, cherished opinions, habits, and behaviors. Our willingness to change allows us to participate in our growth and development with greater ease, with trust in ourselves and confidence in the process.

Step 4

Visioning increases awareness. Awareness changes actions. With awareness, many of our unskillful habit patterns simply fall away. They lose their appeal. Our energies become more focused and the Authentic Self begins to emerge.

Much of our inner growth is accomplished by letting go of that which no longer serves us, including habits, points of view, perceptions, opinions—whatever blocks the next stage of our development. Spiritual growth *is not about getting, it's about letting* ourselves release whatever hinders clear seeing and right action so that we can enthusiastically move forward into living our highest potential.

Step 5

Do you realize you are even now sitting on assets, qualities, talents, and skills that lie dormant within you, or that are underutilized? Step 5 empowers you to at last take ownership of them. Tapping into hidden potential is energizing and leads you into an increase of self-love, self-respect, self-actualization. By acknowledging our gifts and skills we operate from an "I have" mind-set rather than an "I need to get" mentality. It is an acknowledgment of our sufficiency, of the fact that we already have something to contribute.

Step 6

Your sacred "yes" to all that arises in your visioning process amplifies your willingness to do what is required to bring your vision into manifestation. You may support the cultivation of your willingness by recalling moments in your life when you were willing to do something new, to willingly break free from a habit and then apply that energy of willingness to follow through on what you catch when visioning. Then you will discover that when *there is willingness there is a way, but when there is willfulness there is a wall.* Buddhists have a term for "yes" that is very beautiful. It is *tathata*, which means saying "yes" so totally that you become one with your "yes." There is no separation between you and your "yes."

Self-judgment, censorship, guilt trips, or shame cause resistance to opening yourself, especially in steps 3 and 4. Don't judge even your judgmental, resistant mind-set! A "yes" at this stage will soften that resistance. Give yourself an affirmative nod that you are willing to thrive by living the life you have been created to live.

Step 7

Feel, down in your bones, a gratefulness, an appreciation for the vision and for the awareness that it is indeed already unfolding. It is not in the future. Your surface mind may call it "the future," yet even as you read these words it is energetically occupying the space called "you." The vision is already in motion in the mind of Love-Intelligence; it is simply waiting for the fertile conditions to outwardly manifest. By feeling and expressing gratitude, you are acknowledging that your vision already has been activated.

One Last Instruction

Although it is not a formal step in LVP, I strongly encourage you to journal all that comes up for you, beginning with your very first visioning session. This way you can follow your evolutionary progress, revisit insights, set new intentions concurrent with your visioning progress, and observe how the kaleidoscope of your life structures is evolving in perfect sync with your innate impulsion to live your highest potential. Visioning is the means, and authentic self-expression is the end.

Chapter 11

Integrating the Vision into Our Life Structures

I live to be the message that I long to hear
I long to be the way that I'm looking for
I need to shine the light that I want to see.

EVOLUTIONARY PROGRESS WITHIN our eight fundamental life structures is greatly dependent upon our inner ecology, which is determined by the personal code by which we live. It is proactive to examine whether your code of life is influenced by outside conditioning or by your own inner examination of life's purpose, who you are and why you are on the planet, the place in your life of spiritual practice, integrity, ethics, a standard of excellence, inner qualities of compassion, love, peace, joy, selflessness, humility—to name a few. Place yourself on the dot and ask: does my code of living make it harmonious to live inside myself? If your answer is yes, visioning will expand this harmony into one of joyous existence. If your answer is no, visioning will introduce harmony and joy into your life.

The Eight Fundamental Life Structures

You may be asking, "What is the point of stabilizing our life structures?" It is desirable to stabilize our life structures so that they are not impediments to our inner evolutionary progress nor to the development and delivery of our gifts, talents, and skills on the planet. When our basic life structures are stabilized, we are free to devote more time to our spiritual practices, creative endeavors, and selfless service.

The eight fundamental life structures are ego, belief, relationship, body temple, finances, livelihood, spirituality, and community. These are briefly touched upon in chapter 1, and here we will explore in much more depth how they may be stabilized and expanded through the practice of visioning. For this purpose we will look at real-life examples from the lives of those who have been in my classes, clients, and from my personal experience.

Ego

In an evolutionary context, one purpose of the ego was to protect our individual identity, to recognize the difference between ourselves and a poisonous plant, aggressive animals, other tribes that could be dangerous to our tribe—things of that nature. Today's evolutionary progress requires that we transcend the ego and realize our Oneness with all beings, with all life. When we do so, we will cease being frightened by our individual differences, whether they be of race, sexual orientation, or form of worship. We will stop plundering Mother Earth for her resources to satisfy our selfishness and greed.

From an evolutionary point of view, ego itself is not the enemy, but an inflamed, out-of-control ego is one of the most challenging aspects of human nature to reign in, to tame. The root of ego is that we exist as a self separate from the Whole. Relating to ourselves in this way, a "survival of the fittest" approach seems necessary. All this does is give birth to fear, anxiety, mistrust, and greed based on a false sense that there is not enough good to go around so we must hoard and protect how little or how much is in our possession.

The unchecked ego requires maintenance, a constant building up of itself with the props of name, fame, riches, more credentials, possessions, false power, creating castles in the air, all of which can be quite exhausting. Ego keeps us living on the "me plan," including feelings of inferiority and superiority, guilt, shame—and other machinations of the ego which function as a wall between oneself and Reality.

When we stabilize or transcend the ego, we no longer view life through the lens of separation. A healthy ego comprehends the interconnectedness of all life, resulting in wise, generous decisions that benefit the planet and its inhabitants. Softening ego's hard edges enables us to make friends with ourselves, and from there with life itself. With the advent of the global mind created by technology, we are opening our eyes to what it means to be world citizens. People are beginning to make friends with one another all around the world, dissolving stereotypes and prejudices.

Demetria's Dance with Ego

A client of mine, Demetria, had a background in a spiritual teaching that condemned the ego as the root of all evil, something to be destroyed at all costs. Formerly a nun in a Hindu ashram from 1971 to 1981, she was conditioned to believe that doubting any aspect of her guru's teachings was born of ego and a slap in his face, not to mention that it created bad karma. She was told that it would take seven incarnations to reconnect with her guru and qualify once again for the vows of *sannyas*, total renunciation of worldly ties.

When Demetria joined my spiritual community in 1992, she came to me for a counseling session and described how for the first few years after leaving the monastery she felt as though she had received the most dishonorable discharge possible by being sent away from her guru's ashram. She still carried a residue of believing that ego was her ultimate enemy. The conditioning she had received left no space for the healthy ego to take hold, so her self-love and self-worth were quite low. For a few sessions we meditated and practiced visioning. In the questioning segment, especially steps 4 and 5, Demetria was able to touch deeply into her natural essence of humility and separate it from the brand of false humility that was valued in her monastic training.

It is not just monastic training that creates egoic challenges. Any religious fanaticism that preaches we are flawed merchandise due to having been born in Original Sin can also erode our healthy sense of self-worth. Parental and societal conditioning, an abusive love relationship, or working conditions that discount our worth and individual dignity achieve the same results.

When we are asking the questions in steps 3, 4, and 5, if we sit through any discomfort, self-conscious embarrassment, or impatience long enough to penetrate deeply into our core Self, responses will arise that have been long buried in our unconscious. This is why there is no reason to fear what comes up for us, for as we release false beliefs about who we are and who we are not, we free the energy required to hold onto untruths and rechannel it in the direction of awakening to the true Self.

Beliefs

Beliefs differ from a direct realization of truth. Belief is based in the analytical or blindly believing mind, whereas realization is based in the intuitive consciousness. Nor are beliefs synonymous with truth. Beliefs are handed down to us; they are borrowed from philosophies, doctrines, dogmas, opinions, and so on. Nevertheless, it is natural to have beliefs. In fact, sometimes we are afraid not to believe something because we are told the consequences will be dire, like eternally burning in hell or being kicked out of our family home.

The confusion comes when something we believe is challenged by an experience that our belief system insists is simply not possible. We miss many blessings and precious graces that knock at the door of our consciousness simply because they contradict what we have been taught to believe.

Beliefs contribute to the creation of our experience, so it is vital to understand why we believe what we believe. In other words, what is the root system of your present beliefs? Belief is easy; realization requires spiritual discipline. Belief is theoretical, where truth is existential.

Chris Takes a Pilgrimage to His Own Center

Chris was a student in one of my visioning classes. His mind-set—belief system—taught him that God was outside of himself and that he had no power over the circumstances of his life because they were predetermined by the will of God. It was his duty to endure, to be strong and accepting of what he could not change. He was literally frightened that by visualizing and visioning he was going directly against his Creator and possibly facing the torments of hell. Yet I could tell from the expression of hope on his face—and the fact that he had enrolled in the class—that he really yearned to embrace what his inner Self was conveying to him about the true vision for his life. His grief placed him in great inner conflict as his consciousness did hand-to-hand combat with his conditioning.

I first invited Chris to sit with me in affirmative prayer, in a declaration of his dominion over his life which was entrusted to him by Spirit. We then moved into meditation which, as I explained to him, is nonsectarian, as is visioning. He trusted that meditation would lead him on a pilgrimage into his soul, his center of being, so he was comfortable with it.

We began the visioning session with step 2, asking, "What is the highest vision for my life? What is seeking to emerge in my life?" After about twenty minutes, Chris burst into tears. What was revealed to him at first contradicted his belief system, but each time he inwardly asked he received the same intuitive response: he was on the edge of finding a new spiritual path that would accelerate his evolutional progress, and he would return to college for an advanced degree in social work. Then we went to steps 3, 4, and 5. It took a few sessions for Chris to catch the qualities he had to cultivate and release, and identify those he already possessed, and when these intuitions were downloaded, his "yes" and profound gratitude organically followed.

Relationship

In the life structure of relationship, individuals participate in a field larger than themselves. They are supporting one another in the exploration and living of their highest potential. Relationship is definitely on the top ten list of subjects individuals talk to me about, be it about mates, potential mates, family, friends, colleagues, bosses, spiritual teachers—every form of relating in which we humans engage.

Many relationships remain in seed form; they don't sprout when there is detached withholding, withdrawal, manipulation, or control. Relationship is perhaps one of the most powerful sources of our growth. We see ourselves mirrored back with all of our beauty and all of the areas in which we have yet to grow.

How many books have been written on all forms of relationship—how to attract them, how to maintain them, how to grow, nurture, and expand them, how to end and leave them, hopefully in a spirit of friendliness, compassion, forgiveness, and friendship. It was Osho who wisely pointed out that "It is not a question of relationship with somebody in particular. Meditate and find your own center first. Without this, nothing is possible. With it, nothing is impossible." The truth is that every relationship we participate in is a reflection of our relationship with ourselves. After all, we are the only person we can't divorce! Our capacity to relate to others is dependent upon how we relate to ourselves.

Richard Finds His Match

A client whom I shall call Richard came to talk to me about his desire to find a wife. Not one to scour the dating websites, he wanted a more organic approach. When I asked him why he wanted a partner and what qualities they should ideally possess, he wasn't quite clear. So before we entered a visioning session I gave him a homework assignment: first determine your reasons for wanting marriage and then list what qualities you look for in a mate and what qualities you have to offer a mate.

The following week Richard returned with an impressive list which, after reviewing with him, I immediately tossed into the wastebasket. Richard didn't look surprised, and neither was I when he admitted his list consisted of what he was taught as being "right." Not all of what he had written down reflected his own thoughts or feelings—a perfect launching pad for visioning.

We sat in meditation for about fifteen minutes, after which Richard began with step 1, asking about his true purpose in life. Nothing came up for him, so I suggested we sit a bit longer. Suddenly he rose from his seat saying, "No! I really don't think my purpose is to be married. I just caught that I believed I was *supposed* to want to be married."

Richard returned to step 1 and once again placed before his Higher Self the question of what was endeavoring to emerge in, through, and as his life. As he went deeper into a meditative state, an expression of tranquility spread across his face. I thought he had caught a vision, but he just continued sitting in the silence. It's beautiful how individualized the visioning experience becomes, which absolutely increases one's trust in the process.

After a while Richard opened his eyes and silently rested in the energy of his visioning session. When he was ready to speak, he shared that he realized he was gay, that he always suspected this was so but was hiding it from himself. Now that he had formed a loving relationship with himself, it was time to vision for a relationship with a partner.

Richard's visioning was complete with step 1. He needed to be with the potency of this shift in his life before he could move through the rest of the steps. A few months later, when Richard returned, he was all aglow with the beginning stages of self-worth and purpose, so we picked up where we left off and continued moving through the visioning process. The relationship he truly yearned for was to make friends with an essential aspect of himself which his spirit already realized but his conditioning resisted.

Health

A healthy body temple contributes to our being able to fulfill our purpose with vitality and vibrancy. When we respect the body temple by eating a nutritious diet, proper hydration, exercise, rest, and relaxation, we contribute to the flow of harmony and balance throughout our entire system. Physical health alone, however, is not the entire picture. Individuals such as physicist Stephen Hawking, for example, who appear to be severely physically challenged yet live their purpose and contribute a great deal to the world, cause us to realize that who we are is beyond any seeming outer limitation, that we cannot be prevented from expressing our talents and skills.

To be healthy in consciousness, heart, mind, and spirit is equally important to our sense of well-being. Genuine health happens within, not just in our exteriority as a physical body. We are one organic whole, which means that our thoughts and beliefs also impact all aspects of what constitutes health. The absence of illness or physical challenges does not necessarily indicate health, because that is just one aspect of our being. Health is an overall sense of well-being: physically, mentally, emotionally, spiritually. When our physical health is challenged, we can still feel a sense of aliveness, of purpose, of fulfillment. At the same time, we can work with the conscious and unconscious layers of mind and feelings which have a tremendous effect on our physical well-being.

Donna Recharges Her Kidneys

About six years ago, during a class I was teaching, I invited students to present any ways in which they wanted to be held in the field of healing energy. Donna, who was suffering from kidney disease, asked that the class pray that she be moved up the waiting list for a kidney transplant. Both she and the students were puzzled when I suggested that we take a different approach and vision for the healing of the kidneys she already has. My response was that even if she were to be moved up the list, why not experiment in the laboratory of consciousness and see what could be done about her existing kidneys? Donna reluctantly agreed and the work began.

I asked the class, "How many of you woke up this morning and expressed gratitude that your kidneys are working?" No one responded in the affirmative, so I gave them this homework assignment: every time you go to the bathroom, offer gratitude that your kidneys are functioning, then claim the same for Donna's kidneys. (We called it the PP Prayer—praying while peeing.) After all, prayer isn't reserved for only one room in the house, church, temple, mosque, or synagogue. Bathrooms can be great for praying.

Along with a reading assignment, I also invited Donna to give thanks for her life and all the ways in which she had been graced and fulfilled, and then to shift that affirmative energy to her kidneys. Now, I had no knowledge about how Donna was applying this gratitude practice, but a few months later, she tearfully informed me that her kidneys spontaneously began normal functioning. To the day of this writing she is free of kidney disease!

Donna's experience provides factual evidence for how Life Visioning Process step 6, giving your enthusiastic "yes" to what is revealed during visioning, and step 7, expressing gratitude for your vision, powerfully work on the practitioner's behalf.

Money

I have deliberately chosen to use the word "money" for this life structure rather than "financial freedom," or "financial security." My choice is based on the fact that money is a loaded subject, especially in our Western society where it is considered a bit taboo to discuss. So we bypass this awkwardness by using more socially acceptable vocabulary.

As mentioned in chapter 1, we stabilize our relationship with money by realizing that it is energy which, when circulated, cycles back to us. It is an energetic promissory note we extend with full trust in the laws that govern abundance. Money is perfectly adequate as an exchange for products and services. It is neutral and certainly not the reputed "root of all evil." What makes it seemingly "bad" or "good" is how it is related to and used. A synonym I prefer for money is "currency," as in a current that keeps moving, flowing, circulating.

We have all been influenced by familial and societal conditioning where money is concerned. Even the rich can have a sense of lack and limitation and feel that they never have enough money, whereas a person of more modest income can feel very wealthy. It's relative to the individual. Money issues can tremendously impact relationships when a couple has a different understanding of its place in their life. The relationship to money can also affect organizations and the people who work in them, especially those who make financial decisions on behalf of the company.

Moving the Agape International Spiritual Center

Back in 1998, the property Agape was leasing in Santa Monica was purchased. Once we were informed of the sale, my board of trustees and I immediately began visioning for the best location that would serve our rapidly expanding community. For weeks we meditated, visioned, and visited countless properties. Finally, we were guided to a wonderful facility in Culver City. We had to bring the building up to code and do a great deal of remodeling. We couldn't move in until construction was completed, so from June to November we had to conduct services in a large hotel ballroom while also paying the lease on the new building.

Within a short period of time we spent every dollar we had saved since opening our doors in 1986, so we went into debt to cover expenses. We continued to vision and encourage one another to remain in a field of trust that all of the details were being handled, even if we couldn't see how at the time. Each individual's visioning process is unique, so the responses varied both in content and energy.

In addition to paying the lease on the new building and room rental at the hotel, we also had to purchase building materials and obtain permits so the contractor could begin his work. We had absolutely no control over the city issuing our permits in time for us to open on our twelfth anniversary, nor if the bank would approve our loan application to pay for all these things. My board and I were pressed against the financial ropes, and there were moments when it wasn't clear if Agape would even be able to continue to exist.

Clearly, it was time for us to walk our talk. I called a special board meeting. Some board members felt that we lacked the financial resources and time to meet the city's inspection deadlines to open by November. It was a perfect situation in which to stand by our conviction that Agape had a vision and mission in the world, even though in that moment it felt more like a "mission impossible." In spite of differences about how we should proceed, in spite of not knowing how salaries would be paid, construction costs would be met, permits would arrive on time, we kept returning to meditation and visioning to remind ourselves of why we were doing what we were doing, that a way would be found out of seemingly no way.

From a visioning I had on my own prior to the meeting, it was revealed to me that the quality we were to cultivate was absolute trust that "all things are possible." So, during the meeting, I approached each member, one at a time, saying, "I'm not asking you if we *can* do this, I'm asking you if you are convinced that we can hang out in the realm of such a possibility. We don't have to know *how* it will be done, only if it's *possible* to be done." I asked them to hold that space of knowing without getting into *how* we were going to do it. Finally, we arrived at a consensus: it was not only a possibility, we felt it as indeed already done and accepted it as such.

Our contractor, who was not an Agape member, was also in the meeting. It was a first for him to observe our methods. He knew that we had had two flyers printed— one saying we were going to discontinue our services at the hotel and close our doors until construction was completed, and a second flyer announcing the opening of our new building in November. We came to a consensus that we would mail out the second flyer.

Two days flew by and still there was no indication that we would raise enough money to complete construction by our deadline. Nor had we heard from the bank about our loan application. Finally, on the third day, we got a call from the bank. It seemed that the president had walked by the desk of a loan officer who was studying a file. Upon inquiry, the loan officer said he was working on a loan application from Agape, to which the president replied, "Beckwith? Give it to him." The clerk was shocked and informed his supervisor that he hadn't completed his due diligence. Now, I didn't know the bank president personally. In fact, we had no previous working relationship with this bank. Then, as though that weren't evidence enough of the power of visioning, our building contractor said that he was going to double his construction crew and complete the work without pay so that it would be ready in time for the city inspector to sign off on the job.

We opened in November, albeit with cement floors and no air conditioning in ninety-degree weather. Imagine the joy when thousands gathered to celebrate the inauguration of our new facility. We also paid back every loan, totaling $400,000. From that day onward, when challenges arise, we refer back to that day when our trust in visioning and what it revealed gave us the strength to accept that all things are possible.

Livelihood

Livelihood comes right after money in terms of being a vital aspect within our life structures, because it relates directly to our sense of security. It's a beautiful thing when a person feels they are fulfilling their purpose through their livelihood. This happens most often when our innate gifts have the opportunity to express through our profession. There are also times when what we do to earn our livelihood is satisfying enough, even though it does not make the highest use of our greater talents, gifts, and skills. This illustrates how important it is to discern the ambitiousness of the ego from the work of the soul. We may have come into this world with a great singing voice and aspire to deliver our song on the stage of the Metropolitan Opera. We don't have to be frustrated if this doesn't happen. Perhaps our soul-work is to gift hospitalized children with our song. There doesn't have to be a conflict where our livelihood and larger life purpose are concerned. This is where visioning can inform us and prepare our consciousness to catch how both can work together as one organic whole in support of our overall life purpose.

L. C. Finds Her Creative Livelihood

Agape attracts many creative individuals to its doors. Creativity plays a big role in our community, from our youth up to our seniors. One such individual is L. C., a beautician by day and laughing meditation instructor by night.

For years we would talk about the day when L. C. would honor her calling to teach some form of spiritual practice—she has engaged in many throughout her eighty-eight years of living on the planet. So, on some occasions when we met, we would vision about which of her many talents was meant to be delivered within the larger community. With so much life experience, it took only a few sessions of working with step 2 to capture the vision for the unfoldment of L. C.'s livelihood and creative expression. (And yes, she is also still a beautician.)

I share her story so that the role of patience is underscored, as well as the fact that there is no aspect of one's life or time in one's life when visioning cannot be applied. It's about the intuition, the intuitive faculty, which is always alive within us awaiting our activation.

As L. C. and I visioned over a period of weeks, what ignited her heart was to teach laughing meditation to persons of all ages. She is another example of how we may continue in our current livelihood and simultaneously express other of our talents, gifts, and skills in ways we had not previously imagined possible, proving that we are as limitless as we will allow ourselves to be.

Spirituality

Spirituality does not concern itself with matters of the spirit in simply a religious sense. It involves the totality of our being, including our ultimate nature, purpose, and unique relationship to that which is beyond time and space, the immeasurable, the indefinable Great Mystery. Religions have been created out of our inner impulse to understand our origin, our source, the purpose of our existence, and how to fulfill it.

Some individuals begin their journey from an agnostic position, others determine they are spiritual but not religious, and then there are people who do experience guilt or fear about transitioning from a traditional religious path to one outside their faith. And there are also those who maintain both with grace and ease.

The Reverend Dean Lawrence E. Carter Sr., PhD, DD, DH, DRS, DHC

My dear friend and spiritual brother, Rev. Dean Lawrence Edward Carter Sr., founding dean of the Martin Luther King Jr. International Chapel at Morehouse College, has served as Professor of Philosophy and Religion, college archivist, and curator for the last thirty-two years.

The year was 1999, and I had just returned from a conference in the Bahamas when Dean Carter was a guest speaker at Holman Methodist Church in Los Angeles. I succeeded in convincing him to stay an extra night so that we could catch up with each other. As he himself tells it, while attending my Wednesday night service, whose topic was "The Authentic Life," something shifted within him. Following my talk, I invited Lawrence up to the dais to introduce him to the community. As he approached, I saw a glow in his expression that struck me as being more than insight—it was revelation. Following the service he told me, "As I walked up to the stage I knew something had powerfully snapped in me!"

Upon returning to Atlanta and to the Morehouse campus, the first person Dean Carter encountered was his secretary. Standing together in the entrance to his office, he observed that she was staring at him with a somewhat perplexed expression on her face. When he asked her if something was wrong, she responded, "There's something different about you." He inquired if this something were bad or good, and she said, "Definitely good! You're not as pushy as you were." As he walked around the campus, nearly everyone with whom he came in contact validated that there was something about him that had obviously changed.

After a period of self-contemplation, Lawrence realized that he was no longer trying to make something happen, that a new feeling tone of going with the flow and flowing with the go had overtaken him. A new level of trust had been reached in his connection to Spirit. Now, as a Baptist minister, the idea of no longer beseeching a God outside of himself was quite new. The universal principles of unconditional love, of being able to directly work and flow with the laws governing the universe, of not having to plead or bargain in order to have a loving, intimate at-One-ment with the Infinite literally thrilled his soul, and he entered his own unique romance with the Infinite.

To this day, Dean Carter is recognized by Buddhists, Hindus, Jews, Muslims, Unitarians, and Christians of many denominations as the most ecumenical minister in the city of Atlanta, Georgia. Herein lies its beauty: Dean Carter identifies himself as a Christian and a follower of Jesus, while simultaneously embracing universal truth principles underlying all faith traditions. In his own words, "I would not be at this point had I not encountered the teachings of the Reverend Michael Bernard Beckwith and the book he placed in my hands on that memorable Wednesday night, *Words that Heal Today*, by Dr. Ernest Holmes."

Community

Among community members there is a beautiful "communion." While traveling and teaching visioning in many communities, be they churches, spiritual centers, businesses, or social service organizations, I have found that most of them have a way of bringing out in us our talents, gifts, and skills, as well as those places in which we have yet to grow. They teach us how our gifts don't belong only to us, but are a source of being in service to the larger community.

Community expands our compassion and takes us into a broader consciousness of selfless service. We grow beyond a "me and mine" or "we four and no more" mind-set into a "we" consciousness which impacts every community in which we are involved—family, the workplace, our spiritual community, neighborhood, town, state—the world.

Social networking has taught us that community can be formed without sharing a physical location. From sources available on the Internet we learn of our brothers and sisters throughout the world who would benefit so greatly from our support, be it mental, financial, medical, and so forth. We have no shortage of opportunities to contribute our gifts, talents, monetary resources, time, and energies to being a beneficial presence on the planet.

At Agape, for example, we have what's called the Common Unity Ministry, which is the umbrella under which some of our socially conscious programs operate. One of them is Sacred Service Saturday, where our community members come together and, in partnership with other social service organizations, clean up beaches, paint children's summer camps, schools, and hospices, and participate in many other activities. Afterward we gather back at Agape, where individuals share how being of service affected them. Among the many tears of gratitude for the experience is not only how individual hearts opened, but how an emergence of the cosmic heart took over. Oftentimes a whole new world opens, inspiring individuals to return to their own community and enthuse others to a life of givingness. Will you be next?

Epilogue

A View from the Heart

YOU ARE WHAT happens when the clarity of visioning and your life come together for the emergence of your evolutionary potential. However long you have been gracing the planet, visioning your life's purpose will carry you on currents of new inspiration and an awakened enthusiasm will infuse your life structures.

If you are passionate about what is possible for your life, visioning will be a wise guide on your journey. If you are stuck in impossibility thinking, by giving your consent to the momentum of visioning you are saying "yes" to what is actually possible. Remember the words of the wise Queen in Lewis Carroll's *Alice in Wonderland*:

> "There is no use in trying," said Alice; "one can't believe impossible things."
>
> "I dare say you haven't had much practice," said the Queen. "When I was your age, I always did it for half

an hour a day. Why sometimes I've believed in as many as six impossible things before breakfast."

And have fun! A sense of humor about ourselves brings gentleness and humility to the journey. Humor on the path makes it what I call a "blissipline" as well as a discipline. Laugh a lot, and sincerely, because that is the pure sound of your soul. A sense of humor keeps us healthy and belongs in our spiritual practices. In moments or seconds of a good belly laugh we loosen up the ego. Humor is also a vital part of intelligence, causing us to move in the direction of joy and zest for life. Consider the images of the smiling Buddha and how his countenance transmits comfort, hope, trust, and lightheartedness. It's said that that the Buddha cultivated his sense of humor to such a high degree that his detractors couldn't help laughing at themselves. That is how we, too, can lighten up and be a friend to ourselves in both good and challenging times. With humor we move in the direction of authentic happiness. So, remember that it's never too late to begin and include a sense of humor in your practice, especially about yourself.

Visioning supports us in catching the ways in which we sabotage our success and in seeing that these saboteurs aren't inherent—they have been learned and they can be unlearned by identifying them. When we vision we open our inner eye to the innate beauty of our soul, coaxing out from ourselves the courage to look beneath our projections and conditioned reactions with a clear view into our purpose, dreams, and intentions, and how they can manifest.

Epilogue: A View from the Heart

By embarking on your visioning voyage, know that you are saying "full speed ahead" and that the laws governing the universe will be set in motion under your direction. What a beautiful thing it is that you have the desire and courage to claim your natural inheritance and take stewardship over your life by becoming more fully yourself. We all have a spectrum of attributes that are uniquely our own. Appreciate the origin of these qualities, for they were breathed into you by Source. What a miracle it is that intuitive wisdom and knowledge download faster than our surface mind can hinder the process, which alone is a sufficient reason to activate our intuition.

As visioning awakens a deeper appreciation for yourself, your inner contentment and tranquility simultaneously multiply. Reaching this place in your mind and heart reveals even more of your natural inheritance. Witnessing your life unfold through visioning, you will uncover your attachments and learn how to no longer let them have power over you. Instead, you will have dominion over your own inner household.

You may want to consider having a visioning partner. A visioning partner can be one or more persons who come together to vision and support one another in intention setting and other steps in the Life Visioning Process. Visioning is a great contributor to creating a vision and action plan for a business, study group, exercise group—every life structure and environment stands to benefit from clarity of purpose and its fulfillment.

Everything within our life structures has the potential to transform us when we know how to properly relate to it.

And that is the main point: to engage with life so consciously that everyone, everything, everywhere contributes to our waking up, to our mindfulness and awareness. Feedback we receive that insults the ego is a blessing; feedback that promotes the ego is an insult to our spirit. When we consider all that enters our experience as being a teacher, we humble ourselves before the teachings that are offered for our greater good. When we are sincere, the more we welcome insightful glimpses into ourselves from visioning steps 3, 4, and 5, and the deeper we will go in our practice. This is how we liberate ourselves and honor the larger vision for our life that is held in the mind of the Ineffable.

And one more thing: simplicity. By having a clear life-purpose, you simplify your life because you recognize what you must release that obstructs that purpose. Your life structures become uncluttered in many ways. You become less speedy, running here and there, spending long amounts of time on the computer assuring your images on Facebook and Twitter are properly maintaining your ego. You spend less time seeking entertainment and distractions to fill an inner void because you are instead devoting time to fulfilling the intentions in support of your vision. You have found a haven within yourself so that, whether you are at home alone or in the roar of the crowd, you hear the sweetness of your inner voice announcing that all is well.

Visioning offers us a limitless view from the heart into our core self. The heart is stretchable, expansive, and generous about what it sees. In it is the spaciousness to welcome all the ways in which we have yet to grow, and no matter how evolved we become, to maintain our teach-ability, our beginner's mind. So I encourage you to return to visioning again and again to make that connection with your Authentic Self, a self whose exquisiteness has no com-petitor, has no limits, and has all that is needed to live a life of incomparable beauty.

Acknowledgments

I'VE BEEN WRITING this book in my mind for more than two decades. Throughout those years, students in my classes, colleagues, and members of the Agape International community frequently requested that the Life Visioning Process™ be available in book form. While my heart fully complied, given my speaking schedule I simply couldn't find long enough blocks of uninterrupted time to sit and write. Today it is my joy to particularly thank four individuals for helping bring this book to life: my dear friends at Sounds True including Tami Simon and Nancy Smith, and to senior editor Haven Iverson for her caring attention to every detail. And great gratitude to Anita Rehker, my longtime editor, who put her whole heart into this book. I also send out appreciation to my dedicated transcriber, Christina Migliorino.

My profound thanks goes to my beloved friends and colleagues with whom I conducted the very first Visioning Process in my living room back in 1986: Joan Steadman; Nirvana Gale; Coco Stewart; Richard (Dick) Stewart; Eunice Chalfant; Deborah Johnson; Naimah D. Powell,

Acknowledgments

MD; L. Celeste Beckwith; William T. Ropple III; and the late Carol Traylor and Patti Ballard—along with other like-minded individuals. The spiritual bond we formed is as alive today as it was then.

I thank Agape's ministers, practitioners, staff, volunteers, Board of Trustees, members of our local and video-streaming community ("love streamers"), and the students who have matriculated through the University of Agape—all of whom continue to practice and prove the efficacy of visioning in their lives. Much appreciation to my friends and colleagues with whom I share membership in the Association for Global New Thought, on the Transformational Leadership Council, and in Evolutionary Leaders.

Last, I thank those who are an integral part of my overall support system, including Michael Donaldson; Mitchell May; Edison de Mello, MD; Sara Soulati; Aaron Glassman; Anahita Glassman; Stephen Lewis; and Roberta Hladek.

Credits

LYRICS AT THE beginning of each chapter of this book are written by Michael Bernard Beckwith and Rickie Byars Beckwith. To order CDs, visit www.agapelive.com.

Chapter 1
Lyrics from "Spirit Says to Sing"
from *I Walk in the Love of God*,
artists: Agape International Choir

Chapter 2
Lyrics from "I Feel Like Letting Go"
from *In the Land of I AM*, artist: Rickie Byars Beckwith

Chapter 3
Lyrics from "I Feel Like Letting Go"
from *In the Land of I AM*, artist: Rickie Byars Beckwith

Chapter 4
Lyrics from "My Connection with God"
from *I Found a Deeper Love*, artist: Rickie Byars Beckwith

Chapter 5
Lyrics from "I'm Changed"
from *I Found a Deeper Love,* artist: Rickie Byars Beckwith

Chapter 6
Lyrics from "I'm Changed"
from *I Found a Deeper Love,* artist: Rickie Byars Beckwith

Chapter 7
Lyrics from "God Will Work Through"
from *I Walk in the Love of God,*
artists: Agape International Choir

Chapter 8
Lyrics from "Something Turned Me 'Round"
from *I Walk in the Love of God,*
artists: Agape International Choir

Chapter 9
Lyrics from "I'm Ready to Listen"
from *In the Land of I AM,* artist: Rickie Byars Beckwith

Chapter 10
Lyrics from "I Feel Like Letting Go"
from *In the Land of I AM,* artist: Rickie Byars Beckwith

Chapter 11
Lyrics from "Do You Wanna to Know the Way"
from *I Found a Deeper Love,* artist: Rickie Byars Beckwith

About the Author

IN THE 1970s, Michael Bernard Beckwith began an inner journey embracing the wisdom teachings of East and West. Sixteen years later, he founded the Agape International Spiritual Center, a trans-religious community whose local membership, video-streaming community, and international friends number in the hundreds of thousands. He later founded the Agape University and cofounded the Association for Global New Thought, and A Season for Nonviolence. These organizations support his vision and mission of a world joined by humankind's highest potential spiritually, educationally, scientifically, governmentally, economically, and socially.

Agape's local outreach programs feed the homeless, serve incarcerated individuals and their families, partner with community service organizations active in children's schools and homes for youth at risk, support the arts, and advocate for the preservation of the planet's resources. Agape's global humanitarian programs build schools, orphanages, hospitals, clinics, libraries, and homes for unwed mothers.

Dr. Beckwith is a sought-after meditation teacher, retreat leader, and conference and seminar facilitator on the Life Visioning Process (LVP), which he originated. He is the author of *Spiritual Liberation: Fulfilling Your Soul's Potential, The Answer Is You, Inspirations of the Heart,* and *A Manifesto of Peace.* He has appeared on *The Oprah Winfrey Show, Larry King Live, Tavis Smiley,* and in his own PBS special, *The Answer Is You.* He has also appeared in the films *The Moses Code, Pass It On,* and *Living Luminaries,* and in a documentary of his own life, *Spiritual Liberation.* Every Friday afternoon, thousands tune into Beckwith's radio program on KPFK, *Wake Up: The Sound of Transformation.*

His humanitarian activities have attracted accolades from many organizations, including *Ebony* magazine's Power 150 Award, *Celebrity Society* magazine's Power in Spirituality Award, the Black AIDS Institute Heroes Award, the Maharishi Award, and the Model Citizen Award.

For additional information about Michael Bernard Beckwith and the Agape International Spiritual Center, visit www.agapelive.com.

Agape Media International

About Sounds True

SOUNDS TRUE IS a multimedia publisher whose mission is to inspire and support personal transformation and spiritual awakening. Founded in 1985 and located in Boulder, Colorado, we work with many of the leading spiritual teachers, thinkers, healers, and visionary artists of our time. We strive with every title to preserve the essential "living wisdom" of the author or artist. It is our goal to create products that not only provide information to a reader or listener, but that also embody the quality of a wisdom transmission.

For those seeking genuine transformation, Sounds True is your trusted partner. At SoundsTrue.com you will find a wealth of free resources to support your journey, including exclusive weekly audio interviews, free downloads, interactive learning tools, and other special savings on all our titles.

To listen to the author guide "A Creative Visualization" or a podcast interview, "The Discovery of Eternal Truth," with Sounds True publisher Tami Simon, please visit SoundsTrue.com/bonus/BeckwithLife.

 SOUNDS TRUE